A–Z

of Italian Motorcycle
Manufacturers

A–Z

of Italian Motorcycle Manufacturers

GREG PULLEN

THE CROWOOD PRESS

First published in 2018 by
The Crowood Press Ltd
Ramsbury, Marlborough
Wiltshire SN8 2HR

www.crowood.com

British Library Cataloguing-in-Publication Data
A catalogue record for this book is available from the British
Library.

ISBN 978 1 78500 487 2

Designed and typeset by Guy Croton Publishing Services,
West Malling, Kent

Printed and bound in India by Parksons Graphics

CONTENTS

Part 1
INTRODUCTION

The centre of Bristol was for many years given over to Italian cars and motorcycles. In the foreground is an early Laverda 750 twin with drum brakes. Behind it is a 900cc (actually 864cc) GTS Ducati, probably the most reliable of the bevel twins.

Italian motorcycles are revered out of all proportion to the numbers actually built. If you exclude sub-125cc machines and post-Cagiva-era Ducatis, only a few thousand of even the most successful models were built, compared to the tens of thousands that British manufacturers produced. Even today, the big four – Aprilia, Ducati, Moto Guzzi and MV Agusta – produce tiny numbers of motorcycles compared to the Japanese. Yet I would wager that as many people would recognize those Italian brands as would know the Japanese big four. That Ducati, in particular, are able to compete with the Japanese across the board is incredible given their size. Yet on racetracks and in road tests across the world, the Italians are rarely 'also rans'. A Honda executive told me a few years ago that Honda is in MotoGP to sell millions of mopeds and scooters in the Far East. Ducati do not sell any small mo-

torcycles, let alone mopeds, and consider building over 50,000 units a year, cause for celebration. As someone at the factory said: 'When we win at racing, it is like everybody who works here is being given a big red parcel as a present'. The Italians can be absolutely ruthless business people, but with motorcycle manufacturing it is always more than that.

Part of this must be that overused word – passion. While top management is often dispassionate and focused on the bottom line, the same is rarely true of the people on the production line. I have been fortunate enough to visit the Moto Guzzi, MV Agusta and Ducati factories, and the enthusiasm on the factory floor is astounding. Italian motorcycles are usually built by people who believe they have one of the best jobs in the world, even if at times – especially during the 1970s and 1980s – there

Moto Guzzi was one of the first manufacturers to offer rear suspension, operated via springs below the engine. Behind is a Morini, Aermacchi and (behind that) a rare Morini 350cc with 1980s' rather slab-sided styling.

The Aguzzi referred to in the main text. Ridden from Italy, which sounds an achievement until you discover that hub-centre steering legend John Difazio walked.

has been friction. But then, that was also true in England.

The other thing about Italian motorcycles is the number of people who have wanted to build them. Initially, I expected to list well under a hundred marques, but quickly discovered there are mentions of almost 600 in Italy. And those were just the people who made formal and recorded plans: many others with a workshop must have looked at one of the many engines on sale as a standalone unit and thought about building a motorcycle. After all, the first TT-winning Norton had a Peugeot motor. Add to that the fact that, historically, Italy has always made fantastic motorcycle components – think Borrani wheels and Brembo brakes, for example, the latter often fitted to the best Japanese motorcycles. Indeed, when Gerald Davison, the first non-Japanese director at Honda, was running the NR500 'oval' piston grand prix project, he was frequently frustrated that Honda Racing Corporation could not build small components as good as those he could buy off the shelf in Italy. So, new manufacturers

found it easy to set up shop, if not stay the course. Many of the manufacturers survived only a year or so, leaving no record of the motorcycles they built. These are listed in the Appendix; but when the years a manufacturer survived, the region they were based in and some details of the motorcycles they built could be established, then they are listed in the main text.

Other manufacturers turned to motorcycle production out of the simple need to protect jobs and wealth creation when the allies forbade them to continue building military equipment after the Second World War. Chief among these are Aermacchi and (MV) Agusta, who have since returned to aircraft production. Even the Vespa scooter was created for the same reason.

Readers may notice that many companies failed in the run up to the Second World War, and that there are an awful lot of 175s. Both are related to the rise of Mussolini's Government: manufacturers that fell from favour found themselves put out of business, and 175s were

Tax and licencing breaks made 175cc motorcycles incredibly popular in Italy, including for racing. This is a MDDS (macchine derivate di serie), which was a sportier but still production machine eligible to compete in Formula 3 racing and production classes in events like the Motogiro.

given huge tax breaks to ensure affordable transport was provided alongside larger motorcycles, which were still largely a hobby for the wealthy. 175s could also be ridden without a licence or insurance. Ironically, it was the post-war swing from fascism to communism that would push Ducati into motorcycle production. It is important to realize how quickly attitudes in Italy changed, swinging after many years of Fascist and Nazi rule to communism almost overnight. When finally liberated in April 1945, the people of Bologna initially took the Ducati brothers off to face a firing squad, proof of how divided the country had become. Bologna city council actually sent a Ducati 900SS to Fidel Castro as a gift, and it now sits in a museum in Havana having clearly been ridden.

Italy has very few natural resources, although it does have healthy deposits of bauxite, from which aluminium can be extracted. Post-war especially, the poverty of subsistence farming quickly gave way to commuting to factories that sprung up to make anything that might create work and exports. A nation used to a short walk into the fields suddenly needed a means of reaching towns and cities, where they might find work, leading to a boom for anybody who could sell them cheap transport. Again, the rules on who could ride anything below 175cc were almost non-existent, meaning this as the capacity many manufacturers focused on. It was also the reason that the famous Motogiro races, touring the public roads of Italy, limited riders to motorcycles of no more that 175cc.

And this is very much the A–Z of Italian motorcycles. There are no scooter manufacturers listed, unless they also produced motorcycles. And those manufacturers who only made sub-50cc mopeds are also absent. The vast majority used the same Franco Morini or Minarelli two-strokes, and were almost indistinguishable from one another. Given that there were perhaps 200 of them, they too have been omitted, unless they were especially important to the UK market or part of the range of a motorcycle manufacturer.

The year that manufacturers were established is also difficult to address with certainty. Whilst Moto Guzzi started as a motorcycle manufacturer, many did not. Early pioneers might have started out as bicycle manufacturers, as did Bianchi, taking the obvious step into building motorcycles when the internal combustion engine came along. Ducati had nothing to do with complete motorcycles until the communists had ejected everybody with the Ducati name from the business. Despite Ducati celebrating '90 years of excellence' in 2017, it was actually 1948 before a complete motorcycle bearing the Ducati name was sold. I have tried to make it clear in the text when a firm built its first motorcycle, while putting the year the

business was established – regardless of what that business was – in the heading. So the founding date I have given for Ducati is 1927, and I have tried to apply this policy throughout.

And, finally, a caveat on completeness. The occasional periodical I publish, *Benzina*, had a reader send a photograph of an Aguzzi that is reproduced here. During a lunch break amble he had stumbled across the bike in 1985, chained to railings in London's Little Venice. A connoisseur of Italian lightweights, he persevered with notes through letterboxes until he found the owner, an Italian waiter. Despite the little fifty being unregistered, he'd apparently ridden it over from Italy about eighteen months previously. Filled with good intentions, my reader paid £25 for the Aguzzi and stuck it at the back of his garage.

With little to go on, apart from 'Ducati' stamped on various components, and the Franco Morini engine labelled 'no3' presumably reflecting the three-speed hand-change gearbox, I approached dating specialist Stuart Mayhew. He has a treasured old book that includes a census of all motorcycle registrations by region in Italy but it had no mention of Aguzzi. Yet he had come across others in Italy as proprietor of Morini specialist North Leicester Motorcycles, so it is not a one-off.

The engine is by the nephew of Moto Morini founder Alfonso, Franco Morini. He started building engines in 1954, and the business grew quickly to make him the market leader in the production of small but powerful two-stroke engines. But all that really tells us is that the Aguzzi is 1954 or later.

The Ducati name is a red herring: Ducati is a common enough family name and appears on plenty of manufactured goods in Italy, and by 1955 Ducati had barely started building complete motorcycles.

So, Aguzzi was probably a dealer, engineer or even a blacksmith hoping to join the big time: unlike the British bike industry, where everything was made in-house, the Italians bought-in pretty much everything, so setting up as a motorcycle manufacturer was comparatively straightforward. The headlight fittings have shades of Meccanica Verghera (MV) lightweights, and the frame design definitely nods towards Ducati's 98; beyond that nothing is known, so it cannot get an entry in the main text of this book. But it is an admission that while this should be the most complete A–Z of Italian motorcycles in print, there will be marques omitted that never got beyond building a handful of motorcycles before disappearing without trace. Aguzzi was one of them, but at least gets listed in the Appendix at the end of this book.

The other thing that made starting a motorcycle manufacturing business easy, at least until the Japanese

**Laverda's mighty Jota was named in England by Roger Slater – the Italian language doesn't feature a letter J.
The 3-cylinder engine in the Benelli Tornado Tre was originally intended for a new Laverda.**

came along with their mass production and economies of scale, was that it was often very easy to buy in complete engines, the most complex part of a motorcycle. It is also clear what a strong link the Italians used to have with Britain, regularly using JAP, Blackburne, Rudge Python and Villiers' engines. From Germany came Sachs and Küchen engines. From France there were Chaise and Train. Within Italy, too, there were the hugely popular Minarelli and Franco Morini small-capacity, two-stroke singles, as well as, later on, Villa. In the pre-war period, small manufacturers would often sell engines along with complete motorcycles, and those engines could find their way into boat or farm machinery. Indeed, Ducati very nearly gave up motorcycle production around 1980 to become a diesel engine manufacturer.

So, of those that follow, this is a reference to each Italian motorcycle manufacturer in turn, with a brief history of how each started out, their most important (if not always most successful) models and their place in history, including racing achievements. There will be few starting with J, K, W, X or Y because those letters are not in the Italian alphabet, which might be a surprise for fans of Laverda's Jota. It is also the reason that the German ILO engines, which many manufactures used, are usually correctly identified, even though the company's logo stylized the initial I to look like a J, meaning that many records describe them as Jlo.

Some marques will be familiar, others never before mentioned in print, in English at least. All, I hope, are interesting and an insight into a country still obsessed with motorcycles and racing them as often as possible.

Finally, a thank you to those who allowed their photographs to be used, most especially Vicki Smith, Mykel Nicolaou and Made in Italy Motorcycles. Thanks also to the Bonham's motorcycle team and others who were able to fill in the gaps in my research and archives.

Part 2

A–Z OF ITALIAN MOTORCYCLE MANUFACTURERS

ACCOSSATO (1973–89)

Founded by Giovanni Accossato in Moncalieri, near Turin. It produced 50, 80 and 125cc off-road motorcycles that won a world championship, three European championships and twelve Italian championships. They still offer motorcycle accessories, especially for racing.

ADRIATICA (1979–80)

Agricultural equipment manufacturers Giuliano and Alvaro Vernocchi established a road racing team and commissioned famed two-stroke engineer Jan Witteveen to build them a 250cc tandem twin in a Bimota frame under the Adriatica banner. This was followed by a V-twin version raced by Randy Mamola and Walter Villa that would be the basis of Witteveen's work for Aprilia. Financial considerations persuaded the Vernicchis to abandon the project at the end of the 1980 season.

AERMACCHI/AERMACCHI HARLEY-DAVIDSON (1945–78)

Founded in 1913, Aeronautica Macchi – quickly abbreviated to Aermacchi or Macchi – was handily located on the shores of Lake Varese in the north of Italy to specialize in seaplanes. They raced against the British Supermarine S4, 5 and 6 (the forerunner of the Spitfire) in the Schneider Trophy challenges of the 1930s in legendary competitions. Aermacchi went on to build Italy's finest Second World War fighter plane, the C205 Veltro.

Demilitarized in the post-war era, Aermacchi – like so many other Italian aircraft companies – entered the motorcycle business, aiming to ride the wave of demand for cheap two-wheelers. Its first designer was Lino Tonti, later to become famous for his work at Paton, Bianchi and, especially, Moto Guzzi. Tonti's stay at Aermacchi was brief but important, partly because he recognized the value of Aermacchi's wind tunnel. Yes, it was Aermacchi, not Moto Guzzi, who were the first motorcycle manufacturer to use a wind tunnel.

From 1945, Aermacchi built a 500cc three-wheeler, the MB1, aimed at the small truck market. Their first motorcycle was Tonti's 1951 two-stroke 125 Cigno (Swan), which had a folding dummy fuel tank to allow it to be ridden as a scooter or a motorcycle. Like many of Tonti's designs, the cylinder was horizontal and, from 1952, doubled up to create a 250cc twin. Despite these advances, in 1955 Tonti was replaced with the ex-Alfa Romeo and Parilla designer Alfredo Bianchi. His first product was the fully enclosed Chimera, powered by a 175cc overhead-valve engine, looking very similar to Tonti's work, with a horizontal cylinder and unit construction. This was not commercially successful but, when shorn of its bodywork to become the 175 Ala Rossa and 250 Ala Verde, a

This is the old Aermacchi factory, now home to Cagiva and MV Agusta. Its lakeside setting allowed seaplanes to be tested and the factory was clearly once hangars.

The styling on Aermacchi's Chimera 250 gives away the firm's aeronautical past and access to a wind tunnel.
KLAUS NAHR

A competition version of the Aermacchi-Harley-Davidson 250 Al'Oro raced by Angelo Tenconi in 1968.
KLAUS NAHR

successful formula evolved based on Bianchi's principles of light weight, compact construction, simplicity of design and ease of maintenance. Like Rolls-Royce he was only concerned with producing a power output, as he put it, 'sufficient for the task in hand'.

By 1957, these sporting models had established the Aermacchi blueprint of a spine frame with an underslung horizontal pushrod single that would last right up until 1973. The racing Aermacchis grew directly out of these humble street bikes, as much to reduce expense as for marketing reasons, but they worked. The company's fortunes took a big leap forward in 1960 when Harley-Davidson bought 50 per cent of Aermacchi, requiring them to build small-capacity 'Harley-Davidsons' for the US market, to fight their British and, soon, Japanese compet-

itors. By the mid-sixties, over 75 per cent of Aermacchi production was being shipped to the US.

Because Harley went racing under American Motorcyclist Association (AMA) rules, they also wanted a 250cc road bike that they could tune. So, Aermacchi's first out-and-out racer was actually developed for short-track racing in the US. Known in America as the Sprint CRS (for dirt racing) or CR-TT (road racing), they were fitted with magneto ignition rather than the 6V battery and coil of European models. Elsewhere it was known as the Ala d'Oro (Gold Wing), the prototype debuted by Alberto Pagani in the 1960 German Grand Prix.

Results were encouraging, and so the first run of production racers was built for the following season, with a 350cc version (dubbed the ERS in the States) following in 1963. These early racers were none too reliable but, in 1966, a revamp brought a stronger five-speed engine producing more power, more reliably. The uncertain handling of the earlier bikes was also resolved with the introduction of a redesigned chassis with a forged tubular central beam. In this guise, the 350 Aermacchi usurped the British Manx Norton and AJS 7R as the machine of choice for the dedicated privateer, weighing a third less and being only slightly less powerful. But the Italian bike's unit construction engine, lower centre of gravity and considerably smaller frontal area, more than made up for this and, although the Aermacchis were never fast enough to seriously test the works Honda, MV and Benelli fours, they still met with considerable success at grand prix level, as well as winning countless national titles. Aermacchi's rider, Renzo Pasolini, finished a strong third in the 1966 350cc World Championship, behind Hailwood's Honda six and Giacomo Agostini's MV Agusta triple, a feat repeated in 1968 by Aussie privateer Kel Carruthers behind Agostini and runner-up Pasolini, by now beginning his term at Benelli. Although Aermacchi never won

a grand prix, there were several second places, including in the 500cc class, in which the bikes competed by dint of overboring to stretch the capacity from 344cc to first 382cc, then 402cc and finally 408cc.

After the Second World War, Harley-Davidson had built their own 125cc two-stroke, the Hummer, based on the same DKW design BSA had also been gifted for the Bantam as part of war reparations. By the 1950s they needed a replacement and knocked on doors across Europe to find a lightweight manufacturer to help them out. Most factories already had loyalties stateside, so Aermacchi was almost Hobson's choice. Initially, the bikes were rebadged existing designs but that changed when Harley took full control in 1974.

Inevitably, the two-stroke revolution had come to Varese, and the advent of Yamaha's production racers especially was matched by Aermacchi's own two-stroke motors and early success with Pasolini, newly returned to the fold. In 1974, Harley then bought the remaining half of Aermacchi's motorcycle business, allowing Macchi to focus on their renewed interest in aircraft.

A fine collection: in the foreground is one of Aermacchi's attempts to hold back the Japanese two-stroke racing machines: a liquid-cooled 125cc.
KLAUS NAHR

ABOVE: **Incredibly versatile, the Aermacchi single was sold as a racer, a sporting roadster and a small cruiser-like version.**

RIGHT: **An Aermacchi in all but name, the Harley-Davidson RR 250 and 350s were developed and built in the old Aermacchi factory.**

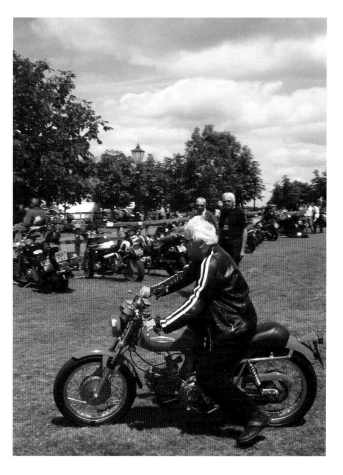

Harley-Davidson intended to get serious about lightweight motorcycles and the European market. Harley could see what the British had missed – that the Japanese weren't going to be happy building small-capacity motorcycles, and were creating a new generation of riders who would start with one manufacturer's lightweight and then stick with the badge on the tank as they climbed the capacity ladder. So Harley wanted a first rung on their ladder and some credibility with a Woodstock generation who didn't get the tough loner image their post-war fathers had craved. Rockers, Angels and black leather were now for a hard-core minority: the rest of the world was in glorious Technicolor, and meeting the nicest people on a Honda. Harley could see the nearly men in Aermacchi's race shop just needed cash and encouragement to be winners. If the old Aermacchi factory could also create a range of two-stroke road bikes to bathe in the race shops' reflected glory, Harley felt they had a plan to conquer Europe and the lightweight market in the US.

Although the two-stroke racers and road bikes were funded by Harley-Davidson, they were really Aermacchi's. The same people were designing and building them in the same factory. Only the money, marketing and road-bike styling came from Harley-Davidson. Despite advertising to the contrary, the new road bikes had nothing whatsoever in common with the twin-cylinder, liquid-cooled racing motorcycles beyond where they were designed and built. The racing would bring credibility that should transfer into sales of a range of half cruiser, half dirt-bike, single-cylinder roadsters.

As well as being nervous about the Japanese moving into large-capacity motorcycles, Harley's shareholders' recurring nightmare was that their heavyweight V-twins were usually bought by older, more affluent riders who might be retiring in the near future. Having acquired Aermacchi's skills and the Varese factory, Harley went about cracking the lightweight market with an advertising budget that set magazine editors' hearts racing. Harley was then owned by American Machine and Foundry (AMF), a huge leisure-industry business whose main income came from bowling alley equipment. They wanted to grow Harley's customer base and reclaim some of the leisure bike market from the Japanese. If they could open up the European market too, so much the better.

The new engines were two-stroke singles in 125cc, 175cc and 250cc capacities, all available as a road or dirt bike, although in practice the difference amounted to knobbly tyres on different wheels and higher exhausts for the off-roaders. The choice of two-stroke engines seems odd today, but was obvious at the time with only Honda building four-stroke lightweights. The rumour mill had it that, like the racing engines, the power plants were Yamaha clones, but it was not so. All the design work was done in-house by the old Aermacchi crew with an eye on future motocross success. The 250cc cylinder head even had a bolt where a second spark plug could be fitted, and the heavy clutches gave away the racing intentions. 'Harley-Davidson' managed a 1978 podium finish in the AMA National Motocross with a 250cc developed in Varese, and the later Cagiva version won a Gold Medal as late as 1981. A double-cradle chassis had no trouble taming some of the lightest bikes in the class.

John Warr, whose grandfather set up the legendary Warr's motorcycles in the King's Road, London, remembers the bikes arriving:

It was great. Harleys are a bargain today, but back in the seventies they were really expensive compared to cars, never mind other bikes. The two-strokes were an affordable way for people to get into Harleys, and we sold loads as second bikes to owners of big twins. They were great bikes — certainly part of my riding education, and I've still got a few. I'm surprised Harley doesn't make more of that part of their heritage, especially the racing success.

Mick Walker, the late racer and historian of Italian mo-

torcycles, imported the bikes to the UK and worked hard to save the Italians from themselves:

The first year the bikes sold well. But problems with quality control meant bad publicity and warranty claims which hit sales. The bikes were also about 10–15 per cent more expensive than the competition. And you got the impression AMF weren't really interested — although Harley had London headquarters, the two-strokes were kept in Whitstable with the bowling alley machines.

Although the road bikes were basic by the standards of most of their competition, things started well in Europe and America. Magazine tests praised the bikes' combination of Italian handling and American looks, and initial sales were promising. They should have boomed when race fans watched open-mouthed as Harley won their four world championships.

Harley/Aermacchi also had a great new rider, Walter Villa, a man Enzo Ferrari called 'biking's Nicki Lauda – a thinking racer'. Englishman Chas Mortimer, a faller in Paso's fatal crash and whose 125 GP record was only recently matched by Bradley Smith, remembers him well:

I'd moved to Italy and lived with Walter and his wife Francesca in the winter of 1969 to 1970. The bike he raced was really an Aermacchi design with the Americans picking up the bills and taking the glory. But some Yamaha parts

The Harley-Davidson Sprint was produced in Varese exclusively for the US market with an electric start.

Two-strokes like this 250cc were intended to replace the expensive to build Aermacchi. Again, all built in the Varese factory that would be bought by Cagiva, who simply rebranded the bikes Cagiva HD.

The brilliant Walter Villa, whose ceaseless testing complimented his and the Aermacchi engineers' natural talents, brought four world titles to Harley-Davidson. Despite Harley running a huge advertising campaign linking the racer to their small two-stokes the public remained unconvinced.
LOTHAR SPURZEM

The frames of the later Harley-Davidson factory racers were by Bimota.

could be used as spares, and Yamaha pistons were found in Pasolini's bike after his fatal crash.

According to Chas there wasn't much to choose between any of the 250s in those days, and part of Villa's success was his constant testing because even small differences could give you an advantage. 'The quick guys came past you on the straights,' remembers Chas, who finished third in the 350 championship in Villa's victorious 1976 season, 'but that was probably because they'd come round the last corner faster than you.'

Villa repaid Harley's cash with interest, landing the 250 World Championship in 1974, 1975 and 1976, the cherry on that final trophy being a matching 350 crown. 1977 was less kind and, although he still managed third in the 250cc title chase, he was beaten by his new team-mate Franco Uncini and Morbidelli-mounted world champion Mario Lega. Perhaps he was less enamoured with the new Bimota frames (at least they weren't made by Harley), although the 350 Yamaha on which Johnny Cecotto won his world championship in 1975 had a Bimota frame as well. For 1978, the 250 and 350 classes were a Yamaha benefit, with Villa only able to take the Harley to sixteenth place, jumping ship to Yamaha at the end of the season.

Yet sales of the road bikes that the racing was supposed to generate ebbed away and, in 1978, Harley-Davidson sold the Varese factory to Cagiva and gave up on lightweights and world championship road racing. Today, Harley-Davidson never mention their world championships, probably because they realize it was really achieved by what was Aermacchi in all but name. Business studies' students must wonder what goes on in Harley's boardroom because, in a nightmare case of déjà vu, Harley bought the Varese factory back from the Cagiva group in 2008 (by then making MV Agustas) only to sell it back to Cagiva for one euro a year later.

Cagiva did show a proposed road-going version of the Aermacchi/Harley-Davidson 250 twin in 1980, but Yamaha killed it with their own 250LC at half the Varese bike's projected price. Cagiva instead turned their attention to Ducati.

AESTER (1932–35)

A Turin factory that built 150cc and 500cc four-stroke motorcycles.

AETOS (1913–14)

These were a handful of motorcycles built by the Pozzi company of Turin powered by a 3½ horsepower 492cc V-twin.

AGOSTINI (1991)

A brief run of 50cc two-stroke mopeds using the Franco Morini engine but with no connection to the multiple world champion Giacomo.

AGRATI (1958–65)

Originally a bicycle component manufacturer that expanded into scooter and moped construction. Also sold under the Garelli name between 1960 and 1965. They were also the importers of many Italian motorcycles to the UK during the 1970s.

AIM (1976–86)

Assemblaggio Italiano Motocicli (Assembling Italian Motorcycles), were based first in Prato, then in Vaiano in Tuscany. At first these off-road motorcycles had 50cc and 125cc Sachs engines. From 1976, mopeds were offered with Franco Morini engines, both with automatic single-speed gearboxes and four-speed manual gearboxes. Eventually, 100cc, 175cc and 250cc models appeared but AIM had to retrench to 50cc and 80cc models, as they fought, unsuccessfully, for survival.

ALATO (1923–25)

131cc motorcycles built by brothers Mario and Giulio Gospio in Turin.

ALCYON ITALIA (1926–28)

In 1910, Cesarani of Caravaggio, east of Milan, started importing French Alcyon motorcycles. Eventually, a 350cc was built under license for the Italian market under the Alcyon Italia banner, initially in Brescia, which had strong connections to both car and motorcycle racing. Production was expanded with a Turin factory from 1925 to include the Alcyonnette 98.

**Garelli were famous for two-strokes long before the sports moped craze. The Ducati is
a 450 Desmo ridden by the author on two Motogiro recreations.**

ALDBERT (1951–58)

Small sports motorcycles, including the 175cc Razzo,
the Gran Sport 175 and 160cc Turismo Sport and Super
Sport models. Based in Milan.

ALFA (1923–26)

125cc and 175cc motorcycles, plus larger capacity models, using JAP engines and Blackburne engines. Based in
Udine in north-east Italy.

ALIPRANDI (1925–31)

Milan factory that used various engines, including 175cc
and 250cc Moser JAPs. From 1928 there were also 350cc
and 500cc models. From 1930 to 1932 they offered motorcycles with 175cc Ladetto, and 246cc and 346cc JAP,
engines with overhead valves under the OASA banner.

ALPINE (1944–62)

One of the first moped manufacturers, based in Pavia, and
also a supplier to other manufacturers of their 48cc two-
stroke engines. This was developed into a record-break-
ing 75cc motorcycle, and finally into a 125cc.

ALTEA (1938–41)

Originally marketed as Sei, after founder Adalberto Seiling – who had also established Motocicli Alberico Seiling
(MAS) in 1922 – and rebranded Altea in 1939. The first
motorcycle was a single-cylinder, side-valve 350cc with
an external flywheel and unit construction, three-speed
gearbox, built in Milan. It was followed by a 297cc side-
valve single and an overhead valve 200cc with a cantilever
style rear suspension. The same engine was also used to
power a small motorboat in 1940 but, due to the war,
Altea closed its doors for the last time in 1941.

AMR (1979–85)

Based in Casarza Ligure, east of Genoa, these were 125–350cc motorcycles powered by German Sachs engines.

ANCILLOTTI (1967–85)

Originally a motorcycle repair and tuning business established in Florence in 1907. A Tuscan factory was built in Sambuca Val di Pesa in 1965, with the launch of an off-road range of motorcycles in 1967. Models of 50–450cc were produced, although it was sales of the smaller motorcycles that allowed production to reach up to 3,000 units a year. Powered by bought-in engines by German Sachs, or Italian Franco Morini, Tau and HIRO motors, ultimately they could not compete with the Japanese.

ANCORA (1923–40)

Based in Milan, motorcycles were originally offered in touring and sports versions powered by a two-stroke 147cc British Villiers engine. In 1924, a new model with a 247cc Villiers two-stroke engine was launched, and subsequent offerings, which included a 175cc and a three-speed 350cc, were in essence developments of the earlier models.

ANZANI (1920–24)

The Italian pioneer Alessandro Anzani began to build engines in France, as did his compatriot Ettore Bugatti. Initially, these were for airplanes and motorcycles but, after establishing a factory in Milan, from 1922 he built overhead-valve, 500cc V-twins, alongside a few side-valve 750cc and 1000cc versions.

APE (1923–25)

Established by Ermanno Agostinelli and Luigi Perone in Cirenaica, in the far south-east of Italy, the name is a combination of the first letters of their surnames, but is also Italian for bee. APE used French 98cc Train engines to offer a sport and touring motorcycle. None are thought to survive. They have no connection to the Piaggio APE three-wheelers.

APRILIA (1960–)

This is another manufacturer that has proved Italian motorcycles can build reputations out of all proportion to their size, especially on the race tracks of the world. Aprilia introduced most people to Valentino Rossi. Rossi joined Aprilia in 1995, winning the Italian 125 Champi-

Aprilia has always been about racing. This is Hungarian Gábor Talmácsi on an Aprilia 125 during the second qualifying session of the 2007 British GP at Donington.
RICHARD MUSHET

onship, and finishing third in the European 125 Championship aboard Aprilia's RS125R. For 1996, Aprilia took Rossi into the 125 World Championship, and began the young Italian's road to becoming the most famous motorcyclist on earth. He finished the season in ninth position, posting five DNFs, but dominated the 1997 season, winning eleven of the fifteen races, to secure his first world championship.

This was Aprilia's sixth world championship, which included three in the 250 class with Max Biaggi. Incredibly, this was achieved by a factory that mainly sold small-capacity, two-strokes and a brace of bigger models that used bought-in Austrian Rotax single-cylinder engines. Aprilia would ultimately win the 125 World Championship ten times, and the 250 championship nine times, including with Rossi in 1999. To date, Aprilia has won 294 grand prix road races, the most of any European manufacturer in the history of motorcycle competition. As well as the rider championships, Aprilia have thirty-eight manufacturers' world championships, across grand prix, World Super Bike and off-road competitions. The switch to Moto2 and Moto3, using a single type of engine, must have been hard for Aprilia's marketing department to bear.

Aprilia was originally a bicycle manufacturer. Established in the wake of the Second World War by Cavaliere Alberto Beggio and based, as it still is, in Noale, not far from Venice. Alberto's son, Ivano Beggio, gained control of his legacy in 1968 and put a 50cc motocross bike into production. Encouraged by its success, Beggio decided to expanded Aprilia's powered two-wheeler range with the first Aprilia mopeds, the Colibri and Daniela, and its first motorcycle – the 1970 125 Scarabeo motocrosser, which continued until the mid-seventies, with versions ranging from 50cc to 125cc. Developed by racer Maurizio Sgarzani, this would become the first road legal Aprilia motorcycle: the 1977 RC125.

In 1977, Ivan Alborghetti also won the Italian 125cc and 250cc motocross championships for Aprilia, moving on to the international stage in 1978 with two podium finishes and sixth place overall in the world championship. This commitment to competition would, more than any other Italian manufacturer, define Aprilia. When Nicolas Terol took the 125 win in the Czech Grand Prix on 15 August 2010, Aprilia became the most successful motorcycle factory in racing history, surpassing fellow Italians MV Agusta with a record 276 victories. Aprilia had

The styling of the Aprilia Moto 6.5 was as controversial as this unusual setting at a Swap Meet/ autojumble.

The V4 version of the RSV was a far more compact and cleverly specified motorcycle than the V-twins; a determined effort by Aprilia to build a fine basis for a racing version.
PIAGGIO/APRILIA

proved that the Japanese could be taken on and beaten. They continued to compete in the 125 World Motocross Championship, reflecting the fact their motorcycle range was mostly off-road models, until 1981, with a best of fifth place in the 1979 season with rider Corrado Madd.

It was this understanding of the relationship, in Italy especially, between road bike sales and racing success that powered the unknown Aprilia on. While the RC125 sold well, Ducati's equivalent, the Regolarità and Six Days 125s, were sales disasters. Ducati might have had the big brand name and history, but Aprilia were the people winning on the track. It helped that the Aprilia was a little more powerful and a bit lighter than the Ducati. But what made Aprilia really special is that it was a young company, employing young people – and most of those young people were designers. Aprilia understood that motorcycles were now aspirational and, other than at their most basic, completely unnecessary. They had to design motorcycles that people really wanted, and then find a way to get them built.

Today it is commonplace to visit, say, the Ducati factory and see crates with the entire rear swinging arm assembly delivered to the factory in one piece, down to the tyre and brake line. Ducati's foundry is long gone, as they too woke up to the idea pioneered by Aprilia – that a

great motorcycle business involves design and marketing, plus assembly of components that have been made elsewhere. Given the superb componentry industries in Italy, it is almost a surprise that it took Aprilia to show the way. While other factories continued to use fibreglass, Aprilia went to find someone who could injection mould plastic fairings. In essence, Aprilia designed first, and then went to find someone who could make it for them.

And so it was with racing. Aprilia already had a relationship with Rotax, having initially bought engines from them, along with HIRO and Sachs motors. And one Rotax-powered motorcycle was doing remarkably well in the 250 World Championship – Cobas.

Antonio Cobas is perhaps the greatest unsung hero of the motorcycle world. He invented the alloy beam frame that is now so universal. He designed the trellis frame, around which Ducati developed their 8-valve range. He was the first to realize that a motorcycle needed more weight over the front wheel than the rear, rather than be shared equally. He realized that a high centre of gravity, and keeping mass as close to the centre of a sports or racing motorcycle as possible, would improve lap times. He realized that long travel suspension could be useful, even on a smooth racetrack. He traded and raced as both Kobas and JJ Cobas, and when he was done with that,

This colour scheme was first used on a production model by Aprilia on a 125. This time it is on a Bol d'Or replica RSV1000R. FL ONE

Repsol Honda snapped him up as a consultant. Yet this quiet man from Barcelona was hardly mentioned when he died in 2004 aged just 52, unnoticed by many. But not by Aprilia, who were keen to take on his 250 grand prix project that had taken Sito Pons to fourth in the 1984 season.

So, for the 1985 250 World Championship, what looked like the Cobas framed Rotax 250 tandem twin with Marzocchi suspension had Aprilia graphics. It was débuted by Loris Reggiani on 23 March at Kyalami for the South African Grand Prix and finished twelfth. Reggiani took podium finishes at Rijeka and Imola, finishing the season sixth, despite four missed races and a DNF.

Reggiani defected to Yamaha for 1986, but repeated his sixth place in the 250 World Championship for Aprilia in 1987, including an emotional first win for Aprilia at the San Marino Grand Prix at Misano. By now Rotax and Aprilia were very much their own team, and ready to start beating the Japanese on a regular basis.

For 1988, Aprilia's 250 became a V-twin, and they backed this up with entries in the 125 class. Corrado Catalano took a 125 podium (third) place in the French round but, like Reggiani on the 250, would finish the season in thirteenth place. It would be 1992 before Aprilia would take their first world championship, although

privateer Andrea Borgonovo gifted them a first (250) European Championship in 1989. But once Alessandro Gramigni won the 125 World Championship, there was no stopping Aprilia. In eight of the next fourteen years, they would win at least one world championship, including a hat trick in the 250 class with Max Biaggi, and winning both the 125 and 250 classes on five occasions.

Back with the road legal Aprilias that the racing was intended to sell, by the early 1980s, Aprilia were offering a range of 125s with liquid-cooled, single-cylinder two-stroke engines, but were still pretty much unknown outside Italy. Then, in 1988 – the year they first entered the 125 Road Racing World Championship – Aprilia launched the AF1. The British motorcycle press were astounded: the specification and appearance was on another planet compared to any other 125cc; indeed, higher than many 1000cc motorcycles. 28bhp would have been respectable for a 250cc not much earlier, and a single-sided swinging arm supported by an aluminium alloy beam frame and full race fairing was unheard of for anything below 400cc. The fact that it closely reflected the specification of Aprilia's world championship 125cc and 250cc racers was a stroke of marketing genius. And while more expensive than the Japanese equivalents, it still looked reasonable value if you really did just want a 125cc sports bike. The Sintesi Replica even came in lurid mauve, blue and red bodywork, later also applied to the RSV1000 Bol d'Or replica.

And then Aprilia almost ran out of steam. Rumours did regularly circulate that a 250cc road bike was inevitable, but when the RS250 finally appeared in 1995, it had a Suzuki RGV engine. Aprilia had been using a 250cc two-stroke single in one of their Dakar-style Tuareg ranges for over a decade but perhaps could see that, given tightening emission restrictions, the days of even mid-range two-strokes were numbered. Some were disappointed, but it was in line with Aprilia's policy of buying in components, so they could at least price their motorcycles at only a modest premium over the Japanese equivalents. The sculpted and polished frame alone looked worth the premium, made for Aprilia by Benelli in Pesaro.

Despite most road tests reporting the peaky RS250 would have been an easier motorcycle to live with had its Suzuki engine not been tweaked, it was probably the nearest thing on the market to a road-going grand prix motorcycle. Unlike its Japanese competitors, the RS250 was also comfortable for taller riders. Today that still holds true for what was arguably the last hurrah of the sports two-stroke motorcycle.

On the grand prix stage, however, two-strokes still ruled the roost. The premier class was limited to 500cc until 2002, which made four-strokes uncompetitive. The maximum number of cylinders was four, so that is what everybody used. But Aprilia and Witteveen had noticed that their 250s could lap faster than the 500s in practice, and that a 500cc twin was allowed to weigh as little as 105kg, as opposed to a minimum of 130kg for the fours. So, between 1994 and 2000, Aprilia campaigned their '500' RSW2 in the premier class, despite it initially displacing only 410cc. The RSW2 was really just a big-bore version of Aprilia's 250cc grand prix winner, and they were not alone in thinking they were on to something: Honda's twin-cylinder NSR500V was also designed on the same principle. But in practice these 'super 250s' would get stuck behind the fours on corners and then left behind on the straights. Later RSW2s were 430cc, then 460cc and eventually 498cc, but were never a real challenge to the 4-cylinders that dominated the era. Aprilia's best result was a third place by Doriano Romboni at the 1997 Dutch TT, and three tenth places in the championship. In a way, it is surprising that Aprilia applied themselves for so long in the 500cc class, given they had no sporting – or two-stroke – motorcycle on sale of more than 250cc.

By the mid-nineties Aprilia were arguably the fastest growing motorcycle manufacturer in the world, building 100,000 motorcycles a year, including the Rotax powered F650 for BMW. This growth was due to, and made possible by, Aprilia's innovative practice of outsourcing production as much as possible. Only directly employing around 500 people, a quarter of Aprilia's staff were involved in design, research and development, or racing. The average age of employees was under 30, so un-

The divisive Aprilia Moto 6.5 designed by Philip Stark. Apart from the headlight layout it is pretty much as he intended. It is a rare example of designers not being constrained by production engineers and accountants, something that perhaps could only happen in Italy.

derstanding what young people wanted and considered fashionable came naturally. Actually making things (as opposed to assembly) was left to others with the appropriate skills and facilities. The best, if not most successful, example of these came with the 1995 Moto 6.5, powered by a Rotax single-cylinder, four-stroke.

Aprilia's first serious foray into four-strokes had started with the Tuareg 350 in 1987, followed by a 600 the following year, joined by the Pegaso in 1990, a bike that looked like it was for off-road use but came with sports bike tyres and suspension: a day to day all-rounder. Hardly heart-stopping, but a solid seller that would be the basis for perhaps Aprilia's most intriguing motorcycle yet.

Phillipe Stark is a French designer, probably most famous for his orange squeezer, a bizarre device that looks as if it came from an alien spaceship and will simply squeeze orange juice on to the worktop below. But he has also designed hotels and yachts, the latter, especially, at odds with his belief that good design should be democratized through mass production. So, Aprilia handed him a 650 Rotax single from the Pegaso and asked Stark to design a motorcycle for everyday use in the city. The Moto 6.5 was the result.

Motorcyclists, especially those in the press, were sceptical. The curved frame tubes would not be as strong as straight ones, and details such as the grey control cables, which would show dirt, seemed dubious. And yet when I took my wife to Paris for a wedding anniversary surprise, seeing the yellow and silver Moto 6.5 for the first time casually parked against the steps at Montmartre, I thought it looked perfect. The market, however, did not agree. Perhaps in today's hipster culture the Moto 6.5 would sell well, but in the 1990s, motorcyclists were more interested in one-piece leathers and large-capacity sports bikes, of which Aprilia had none.

Aprilia's foray into 500cc grand prix racing was even more confusing, given that the class became less popular during the 1990s, largely due to the dominance of Mick Doohan and Honda. Instead people were turning to the World Super Bike Championship, where they could watch motorcycles based on the one they rode – or aspired to riding – on the public highway. Superbikes also offered two races at each round, and seemed to be less stage-managed. The stars revelled in saying or doing something controversial, especially the man to beat, Carl Fogarty, who usually rode for Ducati.

The rules of the World Super Bike Championship allowed 4-cylinder engines a maximum of 750cc, but twins could be lighter and displace up to 1000cc. The received wisdom was that this handed Ducati an advantage, although Bimota and Suzuki built road-going 1000cc V-twins to allow them to enter them in World Super Bike Championships only to find the Ducatis remained dominant. Apart from Ducati, only Honda, with the SP1 and 2, won a World Super Bike Championship by following the V-twin route, and that was helped enormously by Colin Edward's epic riding.

Nonetheless, nobody was really surprised when Aprilia

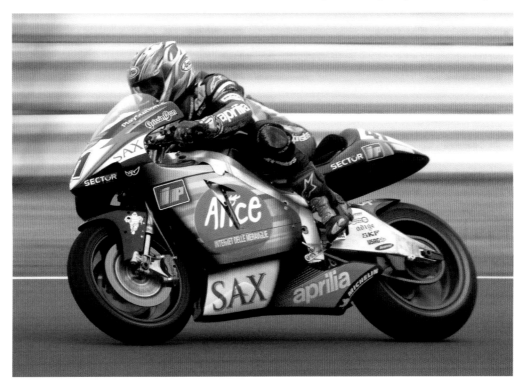

Noriyuki Haga aboard the infamous Cube MotoGP racer at the 2003 Japanese Grand Prix. RIKITA

For some, the Suzuki-powered Aprilia 250 was the ultimate racer on the road. Compared to the Japanese competition, it looked far closer to what was actually being raced by the factories.
SHOHEI NINOMIYA

Aprilia also make some excellent all-rounders. The Dorsoduro is based on Aprilia's world supermoto championship-winning V-twins and was styled by the creator of the Ducati Monster, Miguel Galluzzi, who is head of department at Piaggio.
PIAGGIO / APRILIA

Despite a tiny group of engineers and resources, compared with Ducati and the Japanese, Aprilia are back in MotoGP with a version of the RSV4.
PIAGGIO / APRILIA

announced in 1997 that they were going to launch a four-stroke 1000cc V-twin. Utterly conventional, apart from the 60-degree angle between the cylinders, rather than the 90 degrees used by others, its 998cc liquid-cooled, 8-valve, six-speed motor was as expected. The claimed 128bhp was, however, some 20bhp more than Ducati claimed for their equivalent model, the 996. But the 1998 Mille, as Aprilia marketed it (pronounced mill-ay, Italian for a thousand), looked much bigger than the trellis-framed Ducati, largely a function of Aprilia sticking to their trademark beam frame. But the Mille was much cheaper than the Ducati and also proved more reliable and cheaper to service.

But the Mille could get nowhere near Ducati's success on the track. In 1999, a single Aprilia finished the World Super Bike Championship in fifty-first place, the factory holding back from running a full fctory team until 2000, despite releasing an RSV SP homologation special in 1999.

The 2000 season started well for the official Aprilia racing team, with riders Anthony Gobert and Troy Corser. At the opening round in South Africa, Corser started on pole. At the second round in Australia, he won race two, after retiring in the first. A total of five wins helped Corser to third in the championship. Great things were promised for 2001, and seemed a racing certainty when Corser won both the first round races in Valencia. But these would be Corser's only wins of the season, leaving him to end the year in forth. Ultimately, Aprilia had to admit defeat and walk away from World Super Bike Championships until 2009, when the rules changed to reflect the type of motorcycles people were actually buying. Four-cylinder engines were finally allowed a full 1000cc, and twins 1200cc. Aprilia would be ready with their stunning RSV4.

In the meantime, the new rules in MotoGP gave Aprilia another chance to think outside the box with a 990cc triple. Again, engineer Witteveen was after the best mix of power and low weight (triples could weigh in 10kg less than the 4- or 5-cylinder Japanese rivals), but the RS Cube was far from rider-friendly. Rider Colin Edwards joined MotoGP in 2003 as reigning World Super Bike Champion, his second title. He had beaten Troy Bayliss and Ducati with the Honda SP1, which he lists as the finest motorcycle of his career. He would come to believe the Aprilia Cube was the worst.

He told journalist Mike Scott that:

*The Aprilia was born bad. It was a damn car motor, they'd chopped in half, the chain force was wrong... everything was f***** up. They tried to make it work. It was the future of that time: ride-by-wire, nobody had it.*

As well as being the Piaggio group's sporting marque, Aprilia are also at the cutting edge of styling and graphics, happy to let Ducati stick to the traditional Italian racing red. PIAGGIO/APRILIA

Edwards's best finish on the Cube was a long-forgotten sixth place, and most people remember his heroic leap from a 100mph (160km/h) fireball when the fuel tank exploded. The next year Edwards took a Honda to a rostrum place and started to rebuild his self-belief.

On the drawing board, the Cube was a winner, but in practice Aprilia were trying to make too much of a great leap forward. Derived from a Cosworth Formula 1 car engine, Aprilia complicated development further with a fly-by-wire throttle, a technology still in its infancy and lacking enough subtlety for even the best riders. Other

innovations, such as compressed air for the pneumatic valves, and then additional radiators to cope with over-heating, meant the Cube could not take advantage of a tri-ples' lower weight limit. It produced a claimed 250bhp, more than Honda claimed for the V5 that Valentino Rossi rode to the championship. But the Cube was perhaps the best example, in modern motorcycle racing, that power is not everything if riders cannot exploit it. While Ed-wards is the Cube rider people remember, his team-mate Noriyuki Haga crashed it more often – twenty-eight times in a season.

Aprilia have built many other motorcycles, most very good and carefully targeted at potential buyers, and have always offered a range that appealed to younger and sports riders. Aprilia have never offered a cruiser or ret-ro-styled model, despite hinting that they might when the Mille's V-twin was first announced. This was the rea-son that Beggio decided Aprilia should buy Moto Guzzi, allowing them to sell more laid-back models with Man-dello's transverse V-twins without diluting Aprilia's core values. Better yet, Aprilia would take over in preparation to celebrate Moto Guzzi's 80th anniversary in 2001. At almost exactly the same time, Beggio used his cash pile to buy Laverda, believing the name had a more upmarket resonance that Aprilia and giving him a means of taking Ducati head on in the market place without having to undercut them, which had been necessary with the Mille.

Unfortunately, storm clouds were gathering. Aprilia, like fellow Italian scooter manufacturers Piaggio, were trapped in a spiral of falling sales, dwindling cash flow and heavy debt. Aprilia relied on scooter sales, despite building motorcycles that could win races, because the big sports bikes were generating little in the way of cash flow. Aprilia had an offer from Ducati for Moto Guzzi, but it would have left the very real possibility that April-ia, along with the Laverda name that Aprilia had also ex-pensively acquired, would disappear altogether. As Beg-gio pointed out at the time, 'the proposal presented by Ducati, while much appreciated… is less adequate to the immediate management demands and the expectations of important stakeholders'. So, Aprilia threw their lot in with Piaggio, and Beggio salvaged the title of Honorary President of Aprilia after the takeover.

Piaggio's own problems had started when they had de-cided to invest time and money trying to market expen-sive Italian mopeds to the Chinese. Expanding scooter sales had allowed both firms to ignore their structural mistakes, but the market was about to shrink disastrous-ly. In March 2000, the Italian Government had finally introduced legislation, commonplace elsewhere in Eu-rope, requiring all riders of powered two-wheelers to wear a helmet, where previously scooter riders had been exempt. Historically, fewer than 20 per cent of scoot-er riders had chosen to wear protective headgear and

Aprilia is determined, along with their parent company Piaggio, to see that the brand is strongly associated with racing.

PIAGGIO/APRILIA

with the new legislation rigorously enforced, scoter sales collapsed, leaving Aprilia's new range of large-capacity scooters especially affected. Then, in January 2002, the euro replaced the lira (as it had in some international trading from 1999) and Italian exporters found they could no longer rely upon the quiet but long-term devaluation of the lira to boost exports and deter importers. Worse still, both firms had expanded on borrowed money and reached the point where not only were they struggling to raise new capital, but they also had nervous creditors asking about repayment schedules. In essence, they faced a perfect storm of falling demand, rising costs and an appreciating currency. Through no fault of anyone at Moto Guzzi, their fate was now tied to Aprilia.

Brand devotion was what Italian corporate raider Roberto Colaninno was relying on when he bought Piaggio for $133 million in October 2003. The bargain price tag reflected the sagging fortunes of the marque, immortalized by the Vespa scooter in the 1953 film *Roman Holiday*. In December 2003, Colaninno then used Piaggio to acquire Aprilia and Moto Guzzi in a $200 million deal, although it would not be finalized until the following August. He believed he could restore the Italian two-wheel industry with 'new, top-quality management, and growth allowing us to compete with the Japanese'. Colaninno had worked his way up to CEO at Olivetti and astounded with a $41 billion takeover of Telecom Italia in 1999,

although he was ousted three years later when shareholders backed a takeover by Pirelli. So, in 2002, Colaninno was looking for a new challenge, and Italian motorcycling fitted the bill nicely.

Colaninno's real genius was then persuading creditor banks to swap debt for equity (shares), taking a huge amount of pressure off the group. He also introduced competition among suppliers, and began looking to China for cheaper parts. He allocated each marque a role, Aprilia becoming his sports bike brand. The sportier Moto Guzzis were discontinued, and talk of building a range of V-twins based on the Mille/RSV badged as Laverdas was put on hold. There was certainly enough competition in the sports bike market without creating more in-house. Aprilia, as a dedicated sports brand intending to take on Japanese superbikes and beat them in road tests and world championships, would need something very special. That motorcycle would be the RSV4, announced in February 2008, an out and out sports bike powered by a 65-degree V4 with 999.6cc (just under World Super Bike's 1-ltr limit) giving 180bhp. Even more astonishing was that it weighed around 15kg less that Honda's Fireblade.

The RSV4 made no pretence at being the roomy, versatile superbike that the Mille and its subsequent RSV iterations had been. Unadulterated racing character was matched by features that confirmed its racing intentions.

The Tuono (thunder) uses the same 65-degree V4 as the RSV in a more rider-friendly package. This is the 'Max Biaggi' version in the colours of his WSBK winner. You often see this style of motorcycle parked up in the Italian mountains, their owners casually millling about in a jacket and jeans, ready to show up anybody in one-piece leathers on a Japanese sports bike.

Riders had just about got to grips with highly adjustable suspension and, occasionally, adjustable ride height, when Aprilia offered them variable headstock position and angle, engine height and swing-arm pivot height.

But perhaps the most impressive thing about the RSV4, especially for the price, was the attention to detail and what the industry calls 'surprise and delight' features. While Ducati have quietly cheapened details post the 916 series with, for example, screws where once there were Dzuz fasters, Aprilia have gone the other way. The RSV4 is not just a fabulous motorcycle, it is also a lovely thing to examine in detail.

The 2009 World Super Bike series reunited Max Biaggi with Aprilia, which surprised many who had assumed Biaggi had drifted off into retirement. He only won a single race – at the Czech round – in this opening season, and there was little to hint at what was to come.

Biaggi won ten races in 2010 to become the first Italian to win a World Super Bike Championship. And anyone who knows Italy, will know how much it meant for his win to come on an Italian motorcycle. Biaggi repeated the feat in 2012, after finishing third the previous year. Sylvain

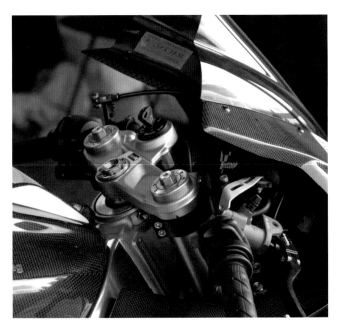

Despite the ignition key, this RSV4 is a track-only motorcycle, the carbon-fibre bodywork one of many expensive modifications to allow it to race at Misano.

Guintoli then won the 2014 championship for Aprilia, after which the race department turned to developing the motor for MotoGP, including revisiting the Cube's pneumatic valves. They will even sell you a 250bhp version for track days at, depending on specification, up to £80,000.

Aprilia's tiny race department – just seven engineers – brought Aleix Espargaro to fifteenth place in the MotoGP championship, with a best finish of sixth. Aprilia have a tiny budget, even compared to Ducati who some estimate have sponsors pay for around 90 per cent of their racing costs. Yet at Sepang in 2016, the Aprilia was only 2.5mph (3.8km/h) slower than the fastest bike – a Ducati at 201.6mph (324.4km/h).

Given their racing success it is perhaps surprising that Aprilia do not have the following that Ducati do among riders and sponsors alike. They have been bold, innovative and successful. And even when things have taken a turn for the worse, failure has never dimmed Aprilia's desire to dust themselves off, start afresh and offer riders and racers alike some of the finest motorcycles available.

AQUILA (1926–58)

Cavani di Bologna, the DKW importer, launched Aquila using 132cc engines from the German manufacturer. From 1934 it added 250cc and 350cc British Python Rudge radial 4-valve singles to its range. Production apparently shifted from Bologna to Turin (or possibly a second factory was established) from 1927 to 1935, including the launch of a new overhead-valve, 175cc sports model. The original Aquila ceased production in 1935,

but the name was revived by Moto Aquila of Rome between 1954 and 1958 to produce mopeds.

ARDEA (1931–34)

Based in Gallarate, where MV Agusta would base themselves, these motorcycles included a Moto Guzzi-like horizontal single-cylinder motorcycle with overhead valves and three-speed gearbox.

ARDITO (1951–54)

Based south of Milan in Stradella, Ardito offered a 48cc moped and a 125cc motorcycle, along with 49cc and 73cc auxiliary engines. From 1953, there was a 100cc two-stroke Sport and a fully faired 49cc scooter with a full fairing.

ARES (1932–35)

A Turin factory that built a small number of 175cc four-stroke motorcycles.

ASPES (1955–84)

Another marque based up in Gallarate, close to Varese. Its origins go back to 1921, when Pietro Aspesi started his bicycle business in the nearby town of Cardano al Campo. Aspes was simply an abbreviation of his surname. After the

An Aspes 125 RGC, Regolarità Campione Italiano 1977 replica.

CJP24

The road-racing Aspes Yuma 125, circa 1980.
PEPROVIRA

war, Aspesi moved to Gallarate and opened a motorcycle shop selling Garellis and Vibertis. When Aspesi's daughter Maria married Teodosio Sorrentino, he was invited to join the family business and help expand it into moped production. From 1961, mopeds such as the Falco were offered, powered by Minerelli engines. The range expanded, aimed at young riders, who increasingly asked about the possibility of a moped with off-road potential. The Cross T – for Teodosio – was the result, and its success determined the future direction of the company.

1970 brought the Apache 125 and the Aspes' tradition of adopting the names of American Indian tribes. Featuring Ceriani competition forks and an 18bhp German Maico disc valve two-stroke motor, it was competitive in off-road competition.

In 1971, a prototype of the 125 Junior Velocita featured the first engine produced in-house by Aspes, with magnesium alloy casings and the crankshaft of the twin-cylinder Yamaha 250. The 1972 Hopi 125 replaced the Apache and also used Aspes' new motor. Development allowed the 1974 Yuma to be the fastest 125cc on the market with a claimed top speed of 85mph (135km/h). Updated with a six-speed gearbox, Aspes launched the first single model race series in Italy between 1977 and 1979. This brought the first chance of fame to riders that included Loris Reggiani, Fausto Gresini and Davide Tardozzi.

Inevitably, Aspes succumbed to the Japanese, with the company being absorbed by Unimoto in 1980, folding itself in 1984. But in late 2008s, the right to the Aspes' name was bought by Menzaghi Motors of Varese, and applied to the Sirio Hybrid 50, a Chinese-built scooter with a Honda-based four-stroke engine and electric motor. It is no longer available in Europe but in China is sold as the Hybrid-50QT-6B scooter.

ASPI (1945–51)

Aspi offered small, clip-on, two-stroke 'Cab' engines to power bicycles and complete mopeds. At the 1947 Milan Motor Show, Aspi (Attrezzature Servizi Pubblici Industriali/Industrial Equipment Services Company) presented a two-stroke, two-cylinder 125cc twin and later showed a rotary valve 175cc, but these were probably prototypes that never reached full production.

ASSO (1927–51)

Produced in Turin by Costruzioni Meccaniche Algadi. From 1931, a sports overhead-valve 175cc, with its single cylinder inclined forward at 30 degrees was produced, joined in 1947 by a two-stroke horizontal single. In 1950, the Ace, another bicycle clip-on motor, was offered.

ASTORIA (1934–58)

Founded near Milan by airman Virginio Fieschi, in partnership with Arturo Rognoni, Astoria manufactured

250cc and 500cc using the Ajax engine built by AJS with four-speed Burman gearboxes. By 1935, Astoria was building its own engines, but folded the following year. In 1950, Fieschi relaunched the marque using the 175 Villiers motor followed by 149cc, 169cc and 199cc two-stroke, four-speed engines designed by Alfredo Bianchi, who would move on the Aermacchi. Similar capacity four-stokes followed.

ASTRA (1931–53)

Astra was the evolution of successful bicycle racer Max Türkheimer's cycle business and he also imported Blackburne-engine, 175cc Stellas. When he passed away in 1936, his cousin, Max Türkheimer Junior, took over the business, but he would perish in a Nazi concentration camp.

Max Türkheimer had imported Hildebrand & Wolfmüller since 1894 and, from 1902, was producing his own motorbikes, using horizontal and vertical single-cylinder engines, branded as Türkheimer. These ceased production in 1905 as Türkheimer focused on the import and bicycle business until launching Astra. This was a Milan factory originally producing an overhead-valve 175cc vertical single, with a three-speed Burman gearbox, upgraded with an inclined cylinder and four speeds in 1934, boosted to 220cc the following year. It was joined by Ariel-powered 250s and 500s, and eventually 350s when Astra produced their own 500cc from 1936 (and 350cc from 1937), as relationships between Britain and Italy cooled. Post-war, the engines were all built in-house, with a 125cc two-stroke and 250cc, 350cc and 500cc overhead-valve singles from 1949.

ATALA (1923–34)

The Milanese-based Officina Meccanica Atala was founded in 1909 by Emerico Steiner. Although the company initially made bicycles, they decided to develop a motorcycle in 1919. The first public appearance was at the Milan Motor Show in 1924, when a 124cc two-stroke motorcycle made its debut with a horizontal single-cylinder engine of Atala's own design. In 1925, this interesting machine raced at the Circuito del Lario (aka the Italian TT, up above Lake Como). The small Atala was a sales success and the company decided to expand the line

with bigger models, using British engines from JAP (initially 175cc and later 500cc) and Blackburne (350cc). The JAP overhead-valve engine was very much a long-stroke motor at 55 × 73mm and featured twin exhaust ports. The three-speed gearbox was by Albion. There was also a side-valve Turismo version. In 1934, Atala ceased production of motorcycles, considering the market saturated and bicycles sales far more profitable. In 1938, the company was bought by Cesare Rizzato, who kept bicycle production going and, after the war, produced several lightweight mopeds and motorcycles under the names Atala, Rizzato and Atala-Rizzato.

ATTOLINI (1920–23)

Based in Spineda, between Bologna and Milan, Gustavo Attolini's small factory fitted 269cc Villiers two-strokes to motorcycles with rear suspension – unusual at the time. There is also mention later of a 330cc two-stroke, perhaps even built in-house. Gustavo's son Gino raced in Milan motorcycle club events, and is on record as a podium finisher.

AUGUSTA (1924–33)

Powered by a 350cc overhead cam motor with a three-speed transmission designed by Angelo Blatto. In 1926, he moved the factory from Turin to Bologna and changed the name to FIAB (Fabbrica Italiana Augusta Bologna). From 1927, 125cc and 175cc singles were launched in Turismo, Corsa su Strada and Corsa su Pista versions (touring, road racing and track racing) followed by a 250cc. The 175cc would gain an overhead cam before the factory folded.

AZZARITI (1933–34)

In 1931, Vincenzo Azzariti designed and built a 175cc engine with desmodromic overhead valves. By 1934, this had been doubled up to create a parallel twin with gear drive to the camshaft, desmodromic valve control and 344cc from a bore and stroke of 62 × 57mm: almost square for the period, and a specification astoundingly close to the 1960 racer that Ducati built for Mike Hailwood. Azzariti also built a desmodromic head for Benelli.

BARTALI (1953–61)

Bartali built the Marziano, a conventional 160cc two-strokes with four-speed gearboxes built in Florence. The Marziano was marketed as a competition model and there was also a moped. From 1955 these were joined by a four-stroke 175cc motorcycle, with a single-cylinder, four-stroke engine and, eventually, a 125cc two-stroke, the Gabbiano.

BASIGLI (1952)

Probably only ever existing as a prototype, it is worth mentioning because the planned motorcycle had a rotary (Wankel) engine, and was perhaps the first attempt to commercialize the idea. The invention is credited to German engineer, Felix Wankel, who obtained his first patent in 1929. Developed in the early 1950s at NSU, a working prototype ran in 1957. This indicates how early Basigli was in trying to commercialize his engine, notionally 125cc, although the capacity of rotary engines is notoriously controversial and usually understated. Basigli's liquid-cooled motor had three combustion chambers and was the brainchild of racer Remigio Basigli of Ravenna. He exhibited it again at the 1960 Milan Trade Fair, but without finding a backer to put it into scale production.

BAUDO (1921–31)

Antonio Baudo's Turin factory originally offered three V-twins with three-speed gearboxes of 474cc, 668cc and 1000cc. From 1926, there were 250s and 350s with JAP or Blackburne engines. Then, in 1927, with Augusto Monaco joining the business, a Monaco-Baudo badged 500cc single-cylinder, side-valve was added to the range and a prototype supercharged was built. From 1930, Giuseppe Navone was building 350cc Mauser and Chaise engines in pressed steel frames under his own name but built by Baudo. He may also have used Train engines. The Monaco name resurfaced in 1950 with a 125cc two-stroke designed by Vittorio Monaco, but it never reached production.

BB (1927–30)

Established in Parma by Ugo Bocchi, building a 123cc two-stroke horizontal single.

BECCARIA (1924–28)

Founded in Mondovì, between Genoa and Turin, by Beccaria and Revelli. Fitted with four-stroke, 350cc Blackburne engines, or 350cc two-stroke Villiers engines, and three speed Sturmey Archer gearboxes.

BENELLI (1911–)

Benelli was founded by widow Teresa Benelli in Pesaro, on Italy's east coast, essentially to ensure employment for her six sons: from eldest Giuseppe, through Giovanni, Francesco, Filippo, Domenico to youngest Antonio, usually known as Tonio. Initially, it was a repair workshop, especially for cars and motorcycles, but also for things like shotguns and bicycles. Inevitably, this involved mak-

1926 Benelli 147 sport in the foreground, in the Morbidelli Museum. The dropped top rail and fuel tank on the model behind was a common variation that allowed women and clergy to ride without wearing trousers.

The model in the foreground might have a chain-driven overhead-camshaft, but still has exposed valve springs. The military version has the more softly tuned side-valve engine.

ing parts – the two eldest sons having studied engineering in Switzerland. The business grew during the First World War, Benelli's expertise expanding to allow them to repair aircraft engines.

After the war, Benelli eyed the growing market for cheap transportation and, by 1920, were selling a 75cc two-stroke to motorize bicycles. Almost immediately increased to 98cc (by 1921), this engine was powering the first Benelli motorcycle. This was the motorcycle the youngest Benelli, Tonio, started racing in 1923 and he would win the Italian championship in 1927, 1928, 1930 and 1931. These wins were achieved with an overhead cam 175cc and, in 1931, a twin-cam version. By now Benelli, along with Bianchi, Garelli, Gilera and Moto Guzzi, were one of Italy's *Pentarchia* – the big five. At the 1939 Milan show, Benelli displayed their first four, a 250cc racer complete with water cooling and supercharging, ready for the 1940 season. A war that destroyed the factory and led to a ban on superchargers left the project on the shelf until the air-cooled fours of 1967.

In 1949, the eldest brother, Giuseppe, fell out with the rest of the family and left to set up on his own account as MotoBi. The first model was the 98B, a two-stroke with distinctive egg-shaped crankcases that would become a MotoBi trademark. Four-stroke versions followed of up

to 175cc. For 1952, a doubled-up version, the Spring Lasting, was introduced. When Giuseppe Benelli died in 1957, his family decided to rejoin the Benelli, which continued production of the 'power eggs' with Benelli badging. When De Tomaso took over Benelli he badged some of his range as MotoBis, including the Sei.

As with so many Italian factories, a lack of sales led Benelli to the world championship in the hope that racing success would result in a boost to sales that would justify the costs involved. Developing the pre-war liquid-cooled, supercharged four into the air-cooled fours of 1967 was the least of Benelli's obstacles to a return to the tracks, with a shortage of riders blunting the factory's efforts – Renzo Pasolini had to race at Modena on 250cc, 350cc and 500cc versions. 1968 saw Mike Hailwood joined Paso, but it was 1969 before Benelli finally accepted that they needed better focus to win a world championship. Paso and the 250cc were the chosen pairing, but accidents blunted the challenge.

Renzo Pasolini – Paso to friends and fans alike – was a spectacular entertainer on and off the track. Funny on TV, especially when baiting Agostini, he smoked and drank, rode motocross and boxed: the perfect template for 1970s motorsport heroes. He dominated racetracks with a style that stopped spectators' heartbeats at every

MotoBi on the Moto-giro: note distinctive 'power egg' crankcases.
MYKEL NICOLAOU

For the 1959 season, Benelli developed this new, short-stroke (70 × 64.8mm) 250cc engine that produced 33–35bhp at 10,200rpm. Despite the multi-cylinder competition, this 250cc was ridden to a win by Geoff Duke in the 1959 Swiss GP, one of his last wins before retiring. Other riders who rode the works Benelli singles at this time included Dickie Dale, Silvio Grassetti and Jack Murgatroy. BONHAM'S MOTORCYCLES

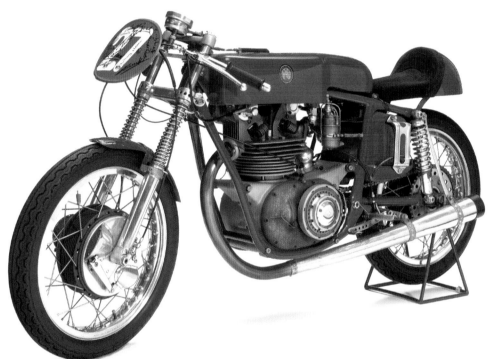

Benelli was sold as Ward Riverside models in the US, available by mail order catalogue on easy terms. This version is only slightly modified for racing. BONHAM'S MOTORCYCLES

The Benelli's valve train. Gears give more certain valve timing than the more common and cheaper chain.

turn. Paso could over-ride his bikes spectacularly, but crashes meant just fourth in the 1969 250cc title chase. Meanwhile, Kel Caruthers, drafted into the team when Paso was injured, lifted Benelli's second and final world championship.

Money trouble led Benelli into the arms of Alejandro de Tomaso, and Paso back to his first love, Aermacchi. He missed the 1972 250cc title by one point, and then 1973 brought the crash at Monza that ended his, and Jarno Saarinen's, lives.

The tragic irony was that Paso might have crashed on oil from Walter Villa's 350/4 Benelli. Pulling into the pits with a leak, Villa was encouraged by his team to cruise home to fifth place in Benelli's last ever grand prix. Christian Lacombe, a journalist worried by the amount of oil on the track, warned marshals who threatened to throw him out of the circuit. Rider John Dodds confronted the Clerk of the Course, and the police were called. So the 250cc race went ahead, and Paso fell on Benelli oil at Curve Grande, followed by Saarinen and others brought down on one of motorsports' darkest days. However, others have said this was all a cover up for Paso's engine seizing, the problem being exacerbated by the need to stop engines at the end of the sighting lap, when the two-

The two-stroke version of the Benelli Leoncino (little lion) 125 won the inaugural Motogiro, but the four-stroke version had this beautiful gear-driven, overhead-camshaft motor. Both had the lion on the front mudguard.

stroke might rapidly cool down waiting for the then compulsory bump start to a race.

Another highlight of Benelli's history was the overall win in the first Motogiro in 1955. This was a 1,000-mile race around Italy on public roads for motorcycles under 175cc, to reflect the motorcycles people were buying in large numbers. Leopoldo Tartarini bought and tuned a 125cc two-stroke Leocini (little lion – a lion was Benelli's trademark) to take a surprise win against serious attempts by the other factories to win the prestigious race that was making the front pages in the Italian press.

In 1972, the marque was bought by Alessandro De Tomaso, a man who divided opinions like no-one else in the Italian motor industry. Some saw him as a modernizer who saved the Italians from themselves, but others believed him to be an asset stripper who took government cash to replace workers with robots. In the 1970s, he owned Maserati, Ghia and 80 per cent of the Italian motorcycle industry.

Born in 1928 to a wealthy Argentinean family, he fled to Italy in 1955 when accused of plotting to overthrow President Juan Peron. Tomaso bought Benelli in 1971, followed by Moto Guzzi in 1973. He believed that 'the Japanese onslaught had destroyed the morale of too many people… then I spent money on equipment. I instructed the design of new models, four-cylinder engines up to 500cc, and six-cylinder for 750cc and 900cc.'

Accusations that the bikes were straight copies of old Hondas were not countenanced: 'Benelli were the first manufacturer to produce a four in 1938, so charges of plagiarism should be directed at Japan, not Benelli'. That must have surprised Belgian firm FN who built a four in 1905, but he did have a point. And the modular approach to design, with many shared parts between models, was revolutionary.

Despite the badges on the tanks, all the four-stokes, including the 6-cylinder 'Benelli' Sei, were built in the Moto Guzzi factory near Lake Como. In fact Tomaso originally planned to badge engineer his new Benelli multis into Guzzis, and there is a four with Moto Guzzi badges in their museum. All the two-strokes – 125cc single and 250cc twins – were built at the Benelli factory in Pesaro, including the ones with Moto Guzzi badges.

Following a stroke in 1993, Alejandro de Tomaso passed control of his interests to son, Santiago. In 1995 Andrea Merloni acquired the brand and launched a series of scooters to give oxygen to the cash registers and organize the sales and assistance network. With this done he was prepared to return Benelli to motorcycle production. The old factory was sold off – it is now a Benelli museum – and a new facility built nearby. While Moto Guzzi thrived with the twins De Tomaso had wanted shot of, Benelli died a slow death.

A relaunch came when the Tornado Tre 900 super sport bike was shown in 2002, and the TNT, roadster some years later. The 3-cylinder engine had been developed for Laverda but as that business collapsed, the Benelli name was revived. Styled by Englishman Adrian Morton, who also works for MV Agusta, the Tre's unique looks with twin underseat fans were perhaps the best thing about

This is Keith Martin, who won a TT aboard a Kawasaki Mach 1. The following year he raced a Sei (both Benelli and Kawasaki were then imported into the UK by Agrati) in the Production and Classic TTs. He wore through the crankcases in the first race and had to work around the lack of ground clearance to make eighteenth in the Classic. Joey Dunlop also raced a Sei at the TT.

The Sei was intended to be opened up to 900cc from the start, and may have had more success if it had been launched at that capacity. The Tornedo Tre was launched in Benelli's traditional green and silver livery, but most buyers wanted red.

the bike. Despite being introduced as a highly priced limited edition motorcycle, it was simply underdeveloped. A cheaper version with most flaws resolved was too little too late and the Benellis could only be sold at substantial discounts. When I last visited the factory it looked to be little more than a warehouse for Chinese-built scooters with Benelli badges. Indeed Benelli is now part of the Chinese Qianjiang Corporation, and, for 2018, Benelli are relaunching in Italy with a range of small-capacity singles, notably the retro-styled Imperiale 400, and larger parallel twins. Other models are available in India, where Benelli are considered to be performing well.

BENOTTO (1947–57)

Another bicycle-maker turned powered two-wheeler manufacturer using various two-stroke engines for a range of moped and motorcycles built in Turin. These included the 150 Dragon and Vultur 125 with three gears, and the Condor, a 100cc with two gears. The final model was the 160cc Centauro Gran Sport with a four-speed gearbox.

BERNARDI (1893–1901)

The Bernardi is considered to be the first Italian motorcycle. It was built in Padua by Professor Enrico Zeno Bernardi, with a four-stroke engine hooked to a bicycle.

BERNEG (1955–61)

Established in Bologna in 1954 by Paride Bernardi and Corrado Negrini to manufacture tin ware for other manufacturers, in 1955 they displayed their own complete motorcycle, the 160cc Iridea. Designed by Alfonso Drusiani of FB Mondial fame it was a parallel twin four-stroke with a chain-driven overhead cam. It produced 8bhp at 6,500rpm. The 175cc Fario (both names are types of trout) was introduced in 1957 with power increased to 11bhp at 8,000rpm, alongside a restyled Iridea. While very similar in appearance, the Iridea had smooth cam covers and unpolished engine side covers. The Fario was available in the Gran Turismo and Normale versions.

BETA (1948–)

Established in Florence by Enzo Bianchi and Arrigo Tosi (their rearranged initials spell Beta), initially building cyclemotors. The first motorcycle was a 125cc two-stroke in 1950, followed by a 175cc sports model that ran in the Milan–Taranto and Motogiro with good results. The 1953 Titan 175 and 125 Urano were the first Beta four-stroke engines. But gradually Beta became an off-road racer, especially with a competitive range of motocross and enduro bikes, during the 1970s and 1980s.

From around 2000, Beta's two-stokes were joined by Suzuki DR engine models, and then KTM powered bikes that returned Beta to significant success in competition, including world trial championships. 2009 saw Beta return to using its own four-stroke power units.

BIANCHI (1885–1964)

Bianchi have made everything from aero engines to trucks, but when Edoardo Bianchi set up shop in 1885, it was to make cutting-edge bicycles: he was first to fit equal-sized wheels, first with pneumatic tyres, first with full suspension (in 1915); and so, when his first motorcycles appeared, it seemed inevitable that they would tread the same path. True to form, Bianchi introduced the first vertical cylinder, the first Earles-type forks and, in 1924, the first bevel-driven overhead cam for the Freccia Celeste. By the twenties, Edoardo was manufacturing market-leading cars and bicycles, and was keen to do the same with his motorcycles. He commissioned Mario Baldi to design a motorcycle that could win the Italian Grand Prix, and the result was the Freccia Celeste (*freccia* = arrow, *celeste* = light blue). All Freccia Celestes were painted in the eponymous light-blue celeste, the colour Bianchi reserved for his racers – including the post-war Giro Tonales and the 500cc grand prix twin – and, of course, Fausto Coppi's all-conquering bicycles. Edoardo said it was the colour of Queen Margarita's eyes, whom he had taught to ride a bicycle.

Although the Freccia Celeste's 348cc DOHC single could make 25bhp and 90mph (145km/h), it was a curious mix of old and new. The semi-unit engine had a dry clutch and quick-release, three-speed gearbox, but it retained a hand-change and a thumb-pushed throttle in an era when most racers at least had twist grips. The twin port exhausts and enclosed valve springs were also unusual at the time, but good ideas that others would copy. Englishman Edward Self (usually referred to as Eduardo in results sheets) used the prototype Freccia to win the Milano-Taranto in 1924.

When Tazio Nuvolari joined the team in 1925 great things were predicted, despite Nuvolari now being 33 years old. He had served as an ambulance driver in the First World War, his fearless style terrifying superiors who clearly didn't recognize latent talent. After the war, Nuvolari returned to racing cars and motorcycles with success, and by 1922 was winning car races (including for Bianchi); but for 1924 he decided to focus on bikes. He settled on joining the Bianchi factory team armed with the new Freccia Celeste. Even though the Bianchi was a 350cc, it could even beat the 500cc on occasion and, especially with Nuvolari on board, it became a dominant force. The 1925 Italian Grand Prix at Monza proved just how dominant it was. The aftermath of a crash in an Alfa Romeo P2 grand prix car meant that Nuvolari turned up to race strapped up in leather and plaster casts. Unable to climb aboard, let alone bump-start the bike, he had to start at the back of the grid and run the 300km (485 miles) race with an oversized

Bianchi racers were almost unbeatable in their day, helped by Tazio Nuvolari who is certainly a candidate for greatest of all time. He won both the motorcycle and car European championships.

Bianchi 175 Tonale MDDS. The overhead-cam Tonale was Bianchi's post-war fightback against the new manufacturers who had leapt into the thriving lightweight market. But it was too little, too late and only Bianchi's bicycles have survived. EL CAGANER

A fabulous last hurrah, Tonti's Bianchi 500cc twin was successful, especially in the hands of Derek Minter, despite the factory slowly going bankrupt.

fuel tank so that he wouldn't need to refuel. By the end of the two and a half hour race he needed carrying off, but had still won. The Bianchi would go on to win the Italian 350 GP for five years on the trot, and by the end of 1925, Nuvolari was European champion: this made him world champion in all but name, a feat he would repeat with cars and the Alfa Romeo.

Edoardo Bianchi was killed in a car crash in 1946, his business having survived the war. Whether he might have avoided Gilera and others' mistake of sticking to pre-war assumptions that it was the 500cc that made the most profit, or if he would have realized that it was the 175cc that people wanted, cannot be known. It was 1955 before the Bianchi board realized their mistake and allowed Sandro

Colombo to design the excellent 175cc overhead cam Tonale. Its success gave his successor, Lino Tonti, the funding for a 250cc twin-cylinder grand prix machine. The motor proved too bulky and so Tonti built a very similar 350cc version, which proved much more successful. Bianchis scored two second places during the 1961 350cc World Championship, with Bob McIntyre finishing a creditable fifth overall. Silvio Grassetti repeated the performance in 1963 and Remo Venturi finished sixth in 1964.

By now Tonti had also built a 500 class twin-cam racer with a six-speed gearbox, its twin-spark 454cc engine making 72bhp at 10,200rpm. Venturi used it to win the 1964 Italian 500 title, but success in the world championship was scarcer. The best result was second place in the Dutch TT, only beaten by MV Agusta's Mike Hailwood. But it was too little, too late – the Italian Government still had not paid for wartime contracts and only the bicycle division was making any money. A joint venture with Pirelli and Fiat saw car manufacture taken on by a new firm Autobianchi, but it did not last long. Even though Bianchi were successfully subcontracting for Ferrari, Fiat, Puch and Motobecane, only bicycle-building was to survive the circling creditors.

BIMOTA (1972–)

A company that has brought some of the greatest innovations to the market, and success out of all proportion to its size. The name is another portmanteau, mixing the surnames of its founders, Valerio Bianchi, Giuseppe Morri and Massimo Tamburini. It is fair to say it is the latter who had the greatest influence and would go on to stun the world with the Ducati 916.

Yet Massimo Tamburini actually believed 4-cylinder engines were best for sports motorcycles, so it was fitting that his follow up to the 916 was the MV Agusta 750 F4, a distant relative of the first bike he built: a much-modified, ugly-duckling, MV 600 shaft-drive tourer. The largely self-taught Tamburini morphed it into a full-blown 750cc with chain drive, trying ever harder to keep away from the local Carabinieri. But, fed up with being the centre of attention, Massimo bought a Honda CB750, vowing it would stay anonymously standard. And then a crash at Misano changed everything: the guts of the CB750 became a running prototype for the first Bimota, with Massimo persuading his business partners that they should sell motorcycle accessories alongside the ventilation and heating equipment they made.

The Bimota SB2 was the firm's first complete and road-legal model. Tamburini's prototype featured underseat exhausts, replaced by indicators for production. Inspired by the RG500, Tamburini felt the layout was aesthetically perfect, something he proved with the Ducati 916 and MV Agusta F4.

Bimota's first offering was a frame kit for the CB750, the HB (Honda-Bimota) 1. Tested at Misano in 1972, word soon got round that Bimota were the default choice for serious racers. A Bimota chassis helped win four 250 and 350 World Championships for Harley-Davidson and, with Yamaha power, introduced Randy Mamola to European circuits and secured the 1980 350 World Championship for Jon Ekerold.

Yet perhaps Tamburini's cleverest Bimota was the 1977 SB2, featuring the new Suzuki GS750 motor. Despite being a road bike, the SB2's chassis was the most radical on the planet. Variable trail was just the start of Massimo's determination to make motorcycles adjustable, and the birdcage frame was designed to make freeing the engine a rapid, straightforward task, as well as ensuring constant chain tension. The SB2 should have featured underseat exhausts, but these were deemed too expensive, even by Bimota standards.

Massimo's first meeting with the Castiglioni family – Cagiva founders and Ducati owners – came while he was working for Roberto Galina's race team, after an unhappy split from Bimota. If he had only styled the 916, then he would be revered as one of the greats: that he did so much more, remaining modest and thoughtful throughout, might just make him the greatest motorcycle designer of them all, and certainly of his generation.

By July 1984, his Bimota legacy was bankrupt, blame attributed to overexpansion and the loss of Tamburini. Thanks to Italian law's controlled administration, the firm had two years to rebuild, replacing Tamburini with Ducati engineer Federico Martini. Martini didn't just

ABOVE RIGHT: **Spot the difference – a Bimota-framed Yamaha and a Harley-Davidson RR developed and built in the former Aermacchi factory.**

RIGHT: **Another YB4, the DB1 (the motorcycle that saved Bimota) and the V-Due (the motorcycle that bankrupted Bimota)**

The original Bimota Tesi production model. Despite the handlebars being isolated from suspension inputs, the Bimota was very sensitive to adjustment, which held it back in racing.

bring experience of things like designing trellis frames, but his contacts allowed him to build Bimota's latest confection around a Ducati engine in a complete and perhaps surprising change of direction for the firm. In 1984, Ducatis were seen as fine handlers that needed more power and at the time the biggest Ducati you could buy was the 649cc SL Pantah. But this was a stepping stone to the Ducati 750 F1 that was introduced alongside the Bimota DB (Ducati-Bimota) 1, with the new 748cc motor, wrapped in Martini's design, which was the first to use fully enclosed bodywork since the Vincent Black Knight of 1954.

What marked the DB1 out was that it was intended to be homologated for worldwide markets, with emission controls and quiet silencers. Build quality and attention to detail were also remarkable for the era. Exquisitely detailed machining is still a Bimota trademark, and the DB1 had it in spades. It sold well and returned Bimota to profit, allowing them to fund Pierluigi Marconi's thesis ('Tesi') on hydraulic hub-centre steering. Bimota would build prototypes with Honda V4s and a Yamaha FZ750 four, eventually abandoning the hydraulics for push and pull rods before putting a Ducati 400 and 851 version on sale.

Poor Tesi sales and its protracted development meant that bankruptcy once again loomed at Bimota, but the model they had developed alongside the Yamaha-powered Tesi would achieve remarkable success. The YB4 had a more conventional beam frame and fuel injection, and was ridden by Virginio Ferrari to win the 1987 Formula 1 title, the final time it was run, having been won by Honda for the previous five years. Davide Tardozzi then almost won the following year's inaugural World Super Bike Championship with the YB4.

The SB8-R was Bimota's attempt to take advantage of superbike rules that allowed twins to run 1000cc engines rather than the four's 750cc. Using the Suzuki TL1000R engine tuned it had 133bhp and was the first bike to feature a carbon fibre composite frame with a self-supported seat unit. However, its success was limited, as the Japanese fours and Ducati came to dominate the series.

Perhaps the most ambitious Bimota of all was the V Due, a 500cc V-twin, two-stroke motorcycle first shown (including an in-house designed engine – a first) by Bimota in 1997. It featured the first electronic direct fuel injection on a two-stroke, cassette gearbox and dry clutch. Its power-to-weight ratio surpassed almost all other motorcycles. But the first production run of 150 units suffered from a woeful lack of development and Bimota had to buy many back from unhappy owners. Eventually, Bimota had to revert to carburettors, but once gain their ambition had led to financial ruin. Bimota were re-launched in 2003 with little connection to a glorious past beyond a range of Ducati-powered motorcycles that feature the most fabulous detailing, and an evolution of the Tesi designed and built by Vyrus. At the time of writing, a handful of models are assembled in Switzerland and the company is looking for another new owner.

The Bimota YB4 that would probably have won the inaugural World Super Bike Championship if the factory could have afforded to compete at every round.

The Bimota DB5 (2005 on) was part of an all-Ducati powered line-up, and incredible build quality, to machined alloy details in particular, had become a Bimota hallmark. MADE IN ITALY MOTORCYCLES

BIMOTOR (1968–82)

Based in Florence, Bimotor produced sports and trail-style mopeds using Minarelli engines, including the six-speed P 6 engine, with radial head and an improbable claimed 12.5bhp at 12,000rpm.

BLATTO (1924–27)

175cc overhead cam lightweight built near Turin. Founder and designer Angelo Blatto was also involved Augusta, Ladetto and Blatto as well as OMB-Broglia.

BM (1950–70)

BM (Bonvicini Marino) were initially two-stroke motorcycles with an ILO 125 and 160cc engines built in Bologna. Four-strokes followed, of 75cc and 100cc, plus a 250cc parallel twin. However, BM soon focused on 50cc models using Franco Morini and Minarelli engines. One of the final models, the KS50, had a front disc brake – perhaps a first.

BMP (1920–25)

The initials are for Brevetti Malasagna of Pinerolo, a small town south-west of Turin. They built 250cc and 350cc two-strokes with unit construction four-speed gearboxes. See also Perugina.

BONVICINI (1931–70)

Based in Bologna, originally also marketed as Baudo and Meldi, Bonvicini used 500cc JAP engines with a three-speed gearbox with, on at least one occasion, an electric starter – a first in Italy. The marque was relaunched in 1955, building 125cc and 160cc two-strokes with ILO engines. Later four-stroke, four-speed models were the 75cc Lusso, 100cc Gran Turismo Lusso, a 150cc single and an overhead cam 250cc twin. Various mopeds followed and then, during the 1970s, mainly sports mopeds using the Franco Morini six-speed engine.

BONZI & MARCHI (1913–17)

A Milanese outfit that used the 330cc Moser single-cylinder engine, and offered two versions of a V-twin.

BORDONE – SEE NB

BORGO (1906–26)

Founded in Turin by the Borgo brothers and offering an overhead-valve design when side valves would be the norm for years to come. Single-cylinder motors of 498cc, 693cc and 827cc with intake valves over the exhaust. In 1920, a 477cc twin offered. In 1926, having been an early adopter of aluminium alloy pistons, Borgo decided to focus on the design and manufacture of pistons, ending motorcycle production.

BORILE (1987–)

Based in Padua, near Venice, a small-volume manufacturer of off-road and retro-style motorcycles with high-quality components and bought-in four-stroke singles. They claim their first motorcycle, the 500 Piuma (Puma), was the first enduro motorbike in the world to have a perimeter frame in chromoly steel.

In 1997, the B54T was shown, styled as a British classic, English-style of the sixties, using a GM speedway engine with a separate gearbox built by Borile. Various versions followed. By 2004, other models used a Suzuki motor, and 125cc and 230cc models followed.

A move to Milan brought an ambitious expansion plan to build a single-cylinder Scrambler range with engines built in-house, the top end based upon parts from Ducati's air-cooled Desmodue V-twins. For whatever reason, probably not unconnected to Ducati launching their own Scrambler range, these models did not succeed. Borile are now using other bought-in engines in a range of capacities from 500cc down.

BREVETTI – SEE BMP

Borile tried to become more than just a niche off-road manufacturer with this, powered by Borile's own bottom-end mated to half a Ducati V-twin. Almost as soon as it was launched, Ducati launched its own Scrambler, which was available at what amounted to half the Borile's price.

BROUILLER (1926–29)

Motorcycles assembled in Turin with 125cc and 175cc Brouiller engines.

BUCHER / BUCHER & ZEDA (1906–20)

Founded in Milan to build a racing motorcycle with an overhead-valve engine. By 1913 this had a 342cc vertical single with two-speed gearbox. In 1914, it was joined by 499cc and 568cc versions with three speeds. A 900cc Boxer twin was promised but probably never built.

BULLERI (1931–32)

Alberto Bulleri of Pisa offered motorcycles based on the 272cc DKW twin with three-speed gearboxes.

BUSI (1940–51)

Athos Busi of Bologna initially built mopeds with various bought-in motors and, from 1952 until 1964, they rebranded as Nettunia with 125cc or 160cc two-stroke engines and four-speed gearboxes.

CAGIVA (1978–)

Cagiva, owned by the Castiglioni family, was founded with the charismatic eldest brother, Claudio, as the nominal head. Claudio knew how to generate publicity and spoke English fluently, something rare in the Italian motorcycle industry at the time.

Cagiva had grown out of a fortune made via the manufacture of locks, belt buckles, and suitcase and handbag clips, but the family's love was racing motorcycles. The Cagiva name was another portmanteau, blending the Ca from Castiglioni and gi from Giovanni, the patriarch, while va came from Varese, the town where they were based in the old Aermacchi factory, at Schiranna. The Castiglioni's had bought this, along with manufacturing rights from Harley-Davidson after the Americans finally decided they would never crack the lightweight two-stroke market. There are more details of this in the Aermacchi entry.

The Castiglioni's were happy to take on the old Harley-Davidson Aermacchi staff, along with some ex-MV Agusta people, and set about developing racing two-

Cagiva originally intended their Ducati deal to involve supplying engines for a range of Cagivas, the first of which was this 650 Allazzara. Poor sales in the US persuaded Cagiva the future lay with the Ducati name.

strokes with bikes unashamedly modelled on Japanese equivalents, especially the Suzuki RG500. The first road-going Cagiva never got beyond the prototype stage, and was really just to test the viability of putting the old Aermacchi horizontal single back into production. However, this venerable four-stroke could trace its roots back to 1963, so the Castiglionis quickly realized that the simplest option was to stick with the Italian-designed, two-stroke singles that Harley-Davidson had been selling, modesty updated and branded as HD Cagivas. But the scale of the Castiglionis' ambitions included showing a liquid-cooled 250cc road bike based on the 'Harley-Davidson' world championship winners, an idea that was shelved when Cagiva realized how expensive it would be, compared to the Japanese opposition. What they needed was a ready-made and established engine manufacturer, and Ducati fitted the bill perfectly.

Negotiations to sell Ducati engines to Cagiva started with an ambitious plan in 1983 to supply some 10,000 motors a year. In the end, none were provided by Ducati until the sale of the entire business was completed in May 1985, but the effect of Cagiva's interest was almost immediate. Finmeccanica, the government body that owned

Ducati, wanted it off their hands as quickly as possible, because all motorcycle factories – even the Japanese ones – were suffering from a worldwide collapse in demand. But Cagiva pressed on relentlessly, acquiring the rights along the way to names that would include Moto Morini, Husqvarna and MV Agusta.

Cagiva adopted the usual Italian business model of pursuing racing success in the belief sales would follow. Starting with the inherited two-stroke singles in the United States off-road market was first pursued with Ron Turner and Duane Summers developing the bikes with some success.

Cagiva then turned to the world championship grand prix circuits. Randy Mamola was the main rider from 1988 to 1990, scoring Cagiva's first podium result. In 1991, Cagiva signed former world champion Eddie Lawson, who would claim the company's first victory when he won the 1992 Hungarian Grand Prix. John Kocinski would also win at Laguna Seca for Cagiva, finishing third in the 1994 World Championship. But by this point Cagiva realized they were wasting their money, and chose to focus on the World Super Bike Championship with Ducati: the early photographs of

RIGHT: Cagiva pushed hard to make their name via grand prix racing in the blue riband 500 class. They started with an RG500 clone but did develop a very different motorcycle. The Japanese factories would actually help them, keen to have diversity in racing to maintain credibility. This is Randy Mamola, at the 1989 Japanese Grand Prix. RIKITA

RIGHT: Cagiva's 125 Mito (myth) unashamedly melded the looks of the 500cc racer and later the 916cc. Often Italy's best-selling 125cc, it had a single model race series that Valentino Rossi competed in.

their dominant 916 had small CRC badges indicating it was designed at Centro Ricerche Cagiva (Cagiva Research Centre) in San Marino. MV Agustas are still designed there.

Yet despite their racing achievements, Cagiva's Ducati-engined models, starting with the 1985 Alazzurra (arrow) and adventure-styled Elefant, sold poorly outside Italy. Cagiva abandoned plans to launch the Paso and Monster as Cagivas (although they still had the Cagiva elephant logo on components) and granted the Ducati name a reprieve.

Cagiva's most famous model is probably the 125 Mito (myth), which was raced by Valentino Rossi in a single-marque Italian series. Along with the similarly powered Raptor, it is all that remains of the marque. Along the way there have been many fine motorcycles – I especially like the Gran Canyon with Ducati 900 power – including the Suzuki-engined Raptor penned by Monster designer Miguel Galluzzi. But, somehow, Cagiva never captured the public's imagination in the way other marques they were responsible for did, most especially Ducati and MV Agusta. Cagiva have been pragmatic enough to focus on those brands, and let their own name fade.

CALCATERRA (1926–29)

The Calcaterra factory in Milan, founded by Piero Cal-caterra, produced a two-stroke 175cc motorcycle, which had an unusual horizontally split crankcases with the cylinder cast as part of the upper crankcase.

CALVI (1923–24)

Another Milanese factory, this time producing a 280cc four-stroke with a three-speed Sturmey Archer gearbox.

CAPPA (1905–10)

This was the Turin base of engineer Giulio Cesare Cappa and offered a water-cooled, vertical single with three-speed gearbox and shaft drive. It was short-lived because Cappa found fame with new alloys and the Aquila Italiana racing car.

CAPPONI (1924–26)

A 175cc two-strokes built in Turin.

CAPRONI/AEROMERE (1950–64)

Aero Caproni was established in 1908 to develop military aircraft, the first prototype flying in 1911. Caproni built a wide range of aircraft, notably seaplanes and bombers. However, like Aermacchi and Agusta, it had to give up production after the war and turned to motorcycles. First was a 48cc two-stroke moped, then, in 1951, the intriguing 75cc Capriolo (roe deer), with a crank in line with (rather than across) the pressed steel frame, overhead valves, four-speed gearbox and pressed steel frame. Later, some 100cc and 125cc versions were produced. In 1954, the 75cc was doubled up into a BMW-style boxer, still using a pressed steel frame and a final chain drive. By now Caproni was manufacturing the frames for the first Ducati motorcycles, the Cucci-olo and the 98.

Between 1954 and 1959, NSU engine machines were built under the Caproni-Vizzola banner to produce the Cavilux and Cavimax. In 1958, the company changed its name to Aeromere, but its 75cc, 100cc and 125cc motorcycles retained the Capriolo moniker. Production of

A Caproni/Aeromere 125cc Capriolo – another high-quality four-stroke from a former aeronautical business.

motorcycles ended in 1964, and Aero Caproni returned to aviation. By the 1970s and 1980s, their Caproni Vizzola Calif sailplane (glider) was setting world records, and the range included a jet-powered version.

CAPRONI VIZZOLA (1953–59)

Another Aero Caproni offshoot in Malpensa, building pressed steel motorcycles with NSU engines from 98cc to 247cc.

CARCANO (1898–1901)

Founded in Voghera by Carlo Maserati, the eldest of the six brothers who would establish the famous car business. Carlo designed and patented an auxiliary engine to motorize bicycles that were built by Michele and Cesare

Carcano. The later Maserati motorcycles are detailed in a separate entry.

CARDANI (1967–69)

Yet another portmanteau, this time of the first names of Carlo Savaré and Daniele Fontana (of brake fame). Built in Milan with the hope of selling to privateer racers wishing to take on MV Agusta, it was a 497.8cc triple with 4-valve heads.

CARNIELLI (1931–79)

Teodoro Carnielli offered a range of motorcycles with bought-in motors from 98cc to 500cc. These included engines from JAP, Python, and Küchen.

Post-war, they fitted Vittoria mopeds with 48cc Lambretta engines, a sports machine with an NSU engine plus a variety of scooters and own-brand motorcycles with two-stroke engines of 75cc to 125cc. There were also a number of mopeds, including the famous Motograziella.

CARNIELLUTI (1926–)

An intriguing prototype 125cc with a rotary valve head and a geared crank that increased the stroke during the induction stroke.

CASALINI (1939–)

A Piacenza factory that specialized in small vehicles and still makes microcars, having stumbled on the formula in the 1970s with the Sulky, a 50cc three-wheeler that could be driven in Italy without a licence. However, between 1956 and the 1970s Casalini also made a range of mopeds and scooters.

CASOLI (1928–33)

Attilio Casoli's in-house designed and built 125cc unit construction of two-strokes with two-speed gearbox, raced with great success and sold in several versions.

CBR (1911–14)

Founded in Turin by Cigala, Barberis and Ruva to build 250cc and, in 1914, 500cc two-strokes. The latter had the carburettor's intake surrounding the cylinder to preheat the air.

CECCATO (1938-)

Originally based in Montecchio Maggiore close to Venice, Cecceto started making burners for bread ovens.

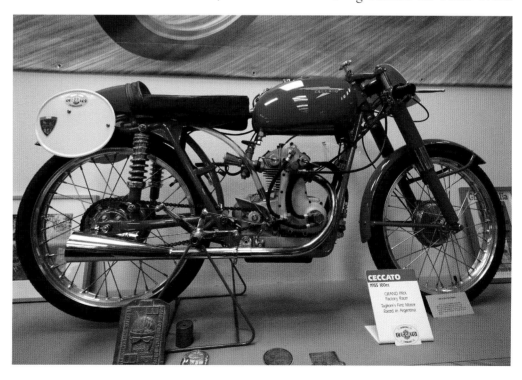

Ceccato 100cc racer from 1955. This was Fabio Taglioni's first engine, developed before he joined Mondial.

But, like so many other businesses in post-war Italy, it saw making small motorcycles as a chance to generate much needed cash flow. As with most others, they started with cyclemotors and mopeds, then two-stroke singles of up to 125cc. There are rumours, but little evidence of, a 200cc flat twin.

Most famous, however, is the connection to Fabio Taglioni. He had designed a twin-cam 75cc engine, hoping to sell it to Mondial. Realizing it was too heavy, especially for long-distance racing, a redesign with a single camshaft drew interest from Pietro Ceccato, who wanted to attach his name to racing success. Over 500 racers were built before production ceased in 1961, although they took two years to sell. Argentina was a major market for the motorcycles, under the Zanella Ceccato banner. Ceccato is now the world's largest producers of car- and train-washing equipment.

CENTAURUS – *SEE MG*

CF (1928–42)

Arduino Castelli and Leonardo Fiorani built an overhead cam 175cc in Piacenza, with a three-speed gearbox. A racing version had a four-speed gearbox and gear-driven overhead cams. The models were uprated to 250cc and finally a 500cc parallel twin. In 1937 they were absorbed by Fusi.

CFG (1926–29)

Colombo, Folli and Genesini built motorcycles with overhead cam 175cc and 250cc singles.

CG (1924–28)

Giovanni Corengia, based in Como, offered 125cc and 175cc two-stroke singles; the latter doubled-up to create a 350cc twin.

CHIANALE (1927–30)

Based in Cuneo in northern Italy, they offered motorcycles with an overhead cam 350cc French-built engine by Chaise.

CHIORDA (1952–57)

A factory in Bergamo, north-east of Milan, that some claim produced a 100cc four-stroke twin, although there is little or no evidence of this; otherwise, 48cc two-strokes.

CIMATTI (1937–84)

Founded by Marco Cimatti, initially producing bicycles and, from 1950, mopeds. In the sixties, larger two-stroke models were offered, including the Luxury Sports 100cc and 175cc, and the competition Kaiman Cross. In the following decade, two 125cc models appeared with five-speed gearboxes, one a motocrosser, and the Aries 5/M road bike.

Between 1966 and 1968, Cimatti won the Italian 50cc Regolarità Championship three years in succession.

CM (1930–60)

Mario Cavedagna's factory in Bologna had a reputation for indestructible engines. Initially, they produced an overhead-cam 175cc with a three-speed Burman gearbox. It was joined over the next two years by overhead-cam 500s and 250s, and finally a 350. In 1947, a new overhead-cam range, the 250 Gheppio, 500 Sparviero and Grifone (kestrel, sparrow hawk and griffon), had four-speed gearboxes. In 1949, CM's first two-stroke was a 125cc single based on the DKW (as was the BSA Bantam and the Morini 125). In the 1950s, this was doubled-up to create a 250cc twin, which was soon improved vastly by changing from girder to telescopic forks and being developed into Sport and SS versions. The final four-stroke came in 1956 with the Francolino 175, and thereafter CM tried to diversify into the scooter market with a 150cc two-stroke. In 1964, CM was taken over by Mauro Negrini to build mopeds but did not survive the decade.

CMP (1953–56)

Based in Padua, they built 75cc, 100cc and 125cc in various trims with two-stroke engines by Ceccato and Sachs. In 1956, a moped and four-stroke 125cc were briefly offered.

CNA – *SEE GILERA*

A 1956 CM 175 Francolino MDDS that competed in two Motogiros. EL CAGANER

COLOMBO (1950–51)

While researching rotary valve engines for Alfa Romeo, Ercole Colombo built a 250cc single with a gear and shaft driven conical valve above the vertical single cylinder. A second version was built, possibly with two carburettors, to test at Monza. Development ended when Colombo died of a heart attack.

COMET (1952–57)

A brand developed under the Brevetti Drusiani of Bologna umbrella by Alfonso Drusiani after he left Mondial. A 160cc overhead-cam, parallel twin with iron barrels was his first offering but was soon replaced by a 173cc version with aluminium alloy barrels. However, the big improvement was an oil pump for the 173cc motor, rather than splash lubrication. A 250cc version appeared in 1955 along with a 98cc two-stroke, but they were not enough to save the company.

COMFORT (1923–26)

Motorcycles built with 350cc engines from Bradshaw,

Barr & Stroud and Blackburne engines with three-speed Sturmey Archer gearbox. All apparently had front and rear suspension, which was unusual at the time.

CONTI (1926–32)

After buying out his partner De Stefani in D & C motorcycles, Vittorio Conti offered new motorcycles with his own name on the tank. Based in Tolentino in eastern-central Italy, they used a split-cylinder, two-stroke Della Ferrera 125cc engine. In 1930, the 175cc Sport off-road model used a side-valve JAP engine. The following year brought the Saetta Azzurra with an overhead-valve 175cc Della Ferrera engine.

CRT (1925–29)

Based in Treviso, the initials stand for Casin and Romin. They built four-stroke Blackburnes of 175cc, 250cc or 350cc, with side and overhead valves, the latter for sports models. All used Druid forks and the Burman gearbox.

D & C (1923–26)

See also Conti.

Tullio De Stefani and Vittorio Conti fitted a bicycle with an old Faini engine, a two-stroke 125cc. Conti first raced this at the Circuito della Stazione in Tolentino, before racing further afield. Thanks to his successes, Fratelli Faini awarded D & C concessions for the Marche and Abruzzo regions. In 1926, they built the MD3-powered bicycle and a touring sidecar version with the Ferrera split-cylinder, two-stroke 125cc that would also power Conti's first bikes.

DALL'OGLIO (1926–30)

Guido Dall'Oglio, ex-of GD, built his own motorcycles in Bologna, with a horizontal 125cc single-cylinder engine and a two-speed gearbox.

DARDO (1926–30)

Built by the Daedo workshops in Turin, it was presented at the first motorcycle fair in Turin in 1926. It has a horizontal single-cylinder engine with two gears and was offered in two capacities, the 132cc Normale and 124cc Sport. In 1928, an overhead-cam 175cc model with a heavily finned cylinder joined the range.

DE AGOSTINI (1925–27)

Motorcycles with twin-cylinder Del Ferrera 125cc engines.

DECA (1955–58)

Based in Borgo Piave, between Rome and Naples, Deca produced a rare four-stroke 48cc lightweight model with three gears, doubled-up to a four-speed 96cc twin. A 125cc version followed and, possibly, two-stroke models.

An all-Italian podium in the winner's enclosure at the Classic TT – two MV Agusta triples, and a Patton twin.

DEI (1932–50)

Founded by Umberto Dei as a bicycle factory and quickly moving on to build lightweight motorcycles with two-stroke engines of 60cc and 75cc. From 1941, a 98cc development had a two-speed gearbox, but still with a rigid chassis. The Saxonette used the 60cc German motor and post-war there was a Sachs 150cc four-speed model. Otherwise Dei then relied on the Garelli Mosquito motor.

DELLA FERRERA (1909–42)

The Della Ferrera brothers would build one of Italy's most important brands in Turin. Hand-built, they offered 330cc and, later, 499cc engines with overhead cams and hemispherical combustion chambers – very advanced for the era. By 1913, a 500cc V-twin joined the range and distribution with overhead valves. The following year the 500cc was relaunched with a 4-valve head and great competition success.

Post-war production resumed in 1919 with a 636cc single and a 1006cc V-twin, both with four speeds. These were offered in a variety of specifications and capacities, including some side-valve models. There was also a small two-stroke auxiliary motor and overhead-cam 175cc and 350cc singles. Some believe the factory did manage to continue until as late as 1948.

DEMM (1953–83)

The Demm brothers of Milan produced small motorcycles with two-stroke engines of 50cc, 53cc and 75cc, as well as overhead-cam models of 125cc and 175cc. They supplied engines only to other manufacturers.

DE TOGNI (1931–35)

A Bolognese concern building a Scott-inspired DKW 175cc-powered, three-gear motorcycle with odd retractable stabilizers. Post-war, it also offered mini-vans with a two-stroke Sachs engine.

DEVIL (1953–58)

Based in Fiorano del Serio, the factory was located in Bergamo with the main office in Milan. Devil was a subsidiary of precision machining firm OCMA, initially manufacturing two-strokes, a 125cc and 160cc for boats, and a 250cc minivan. In 1955, the Devlino moped of 48cc was released. The designer William Soncini was employed in 1956 and designed overhead-cam 125cc and 175cc engines, plus a twin-cam 175cc with potential as a Formula 3 racer. Soncini went on to success at Aermacchi.

DIANA (1923–25)

This was the project of Bolognese engineer, Nerino Ghibellini, sold via dealer Ernesto Pettazzoni: DKW horizontal cylinder two-stroke singles of 118cc or 147cc. Ghibellini raced the Diana at the Circuito del Lario and Motogiro d'Italia, but the business was failing and from 1924 he was simply a repair workshop.

DOGLIOLI & CIVARDI (1929–35)

Overhead-valve 175s built in Turin, initially with Norman engines and later with New Imperial. Subsequent models also used Italian MAS (Motocicli Alberico Seiling), JAP and Rudge Python Rudge engines of 250cc, 350cc and 500cc.

DOMINISSIMI (1924–28)

The Dominissimi brothers' workshop was based in Pordenone, north of Venice. Their models were powered by 175cc and 250cc DKW engines.

DONISELLI (1951–73)

Bicycle manufacturers who expanded into a variety of powered vehicles, using sub-50cc motors from Alpino, Demm, Ardito and Sachs, and 125, 150 and 175s from ILO.

DOTTA (1925–35)

Turin factory offering a motorized bicycle and the two-stroke Piazza 125.

DUCATI (1927–)

There are so many books on Ducati – including one I wrote for Crowood – that there is little that can really be meaningfully added here. A few myths will be dealt with, together with the often forgotten origins of the factory and the fate of the eponymous family who had no interest that we know of in motorcycles. The photographs and their captions will hopefully tell much of the motorcycles' stories.

Ducati was an electronics business, but that part of it was hived off in 1953 and still exists. No motorcycles were built until 1948, by which time the Ducati family had either been removed or had left the company. And while Ducati are often revered, in truth many of their two-wheelers were disasters. There are many boasts, for example, around the Cruiser scooter and its specification, but performance was dire as a result of it being far too heavy and sales were poor. The Muletta (little mule or donkey) was a small, three-wheel truck intended to compete with the Piaggio Ape. It had an expensive to build and maintain bevel driven by Ducati's overhead-cam motor, rather than the competitions' simple two-stroke engines. And the rightly feted Massimo Tamburini penned

the Paso, a motorcycle Ducati's new owners, Cagiva, expected to be a worldwide sales' hit, but it bombed in every market and, even today, can be bought for a few weeks' average pay. Conversely, the Monster, praised at launch but predicted to be a poor seller, as it was not a sports bike or obviously a Ducati, went on to become the bestselling Italian motorcycle of all time. And this despite being originally intended, along with the Paso, to be sold badged as a Cagiva, rather than as a Ducati.

Ducati came into being on the fourth of July – although it's probably simply a coincidence that is Independence Day in the USA – in 1926. Giving the original firm its full name, Scientific Society Radio Brevetti Ducati SpA was established with funding provided by the Ducati brothers' father selling a property in Florence. Antonio Cavalieri Ducati was eager to build a company around his eldest son, Adriano, already a brilliant physicist of note at just 19 years old. Having moved the family from Comacchio, on Italy's east coast, to Bologna, industrial engineer Antonio wanted to make the most of the city's reputation as the hotbed of Italy's industrial revolution. The university was also a world leader in physics and radio telegraphy, thanks to Bologna's most famous son at the time, Guglielmo Marconi.

The original Ducati/ Siata Cucciolo was just a kit to convert a bicycle to a moped. Later, Ducati offered a ready-to-ride version.

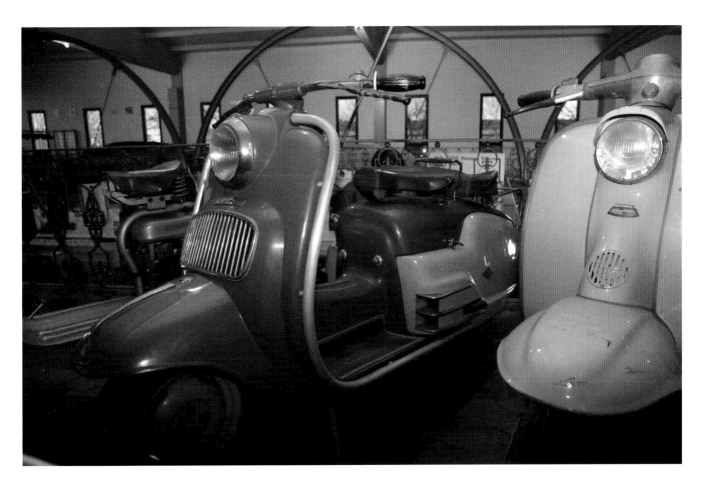

The Ducati Cruiser was an attempt to join the incredibly profitable scooter market, but its specification made it heavy and meant initial acceleration was poor. It was also, inevitably, expensive.

Although Ducati raced their pushrod models (left), it took Taglioni's 100cc and 125cc with bevel gear drive to an overhead camshaft to give Ducati a proven winner.

The final incarnation of Ducati's bevel singles was the 450 Desmo styled by Leopoldo Tartarini of Italjet. He also penned the 750 Sport and SS, and the Darmah.

At Stan Hailwood's request, Taglioni designed 250cc and 350cc twins for son Mike to race. They handled poorly and were too heavy. John Surtees had one reframed for his brother to race.

Adriano Cavalieri Ducati was very much following in Marconi's footsteps, whose new radio equipment would allow a ship, for the first time, to maintain radio contact with all five continents at once. Ducati's first 'factory' was the basement of the family home, with potential clients being invited to 'offices' that were simply three rented rooms near to the centre of Bologna. The business model was to exploit Adriano's patents, of which there were eventually over 200. The first Ducati product was a Manens ('steady') capacitor, and samples were dispatched worldwide in a search for business. Adriano would often accompany them, and seems to have been a gifted salesman, as well as a physicist.

Adriano's brother Bruno was a just a year younger and almost as talented. He had qualified as an architect and so designed and supervised the building of a purpose-built Ducati factory to house a business that had quickly outgrown the family basement. His visionary state-of-the art factory opened in 1935, on the outskirts of Bologna, employing as many as 7,000 people. The area was little more than a village known as Borgo Panigale, and remains the home of Ducati today.

Ducati's wartime history was dramatic; its expertise in electronics so valuable that the Nazis took full control, leaving the Allies with little option but to declare the Ducati factory 'Target 18 at 830513'. Without a hint of irony, it was flattened as part of Operation Pancake.

Post-war, despite Ducati's equipment and stock having been safely hidden away from the factory, there was not a big enough market for their expensive products. For the Ducati brothers, the end of the war seemed to mark the end of their business. They were never paid the compensation due for their razed factory and quickly lost control of the family enterprise. Adriano's genius was, however, immediately recognized. As part of Werner Von Braun's scientific team, he moved to America, and became one of the core aerospace team within NASA that put a man on the moon.

Bologna's communist masters tolerated Adriano's brothers' (Bruno and Marcello) attempts to rebuild their business, because it created work. Initially, they stuck with electrical goods – radios, razors and then even cameras – but it was a clip-on motor that saved Ducati. The Cucciolo (little puppy, after its barking exhaust note) was

Ducati's first V4 designed by Taglioni for a US police bike. Ducati's importer, Berliner (hence the b on the fuel tank), was convinced they could sell the bike but it proved too heavy and powerful for the tyres of the day.

a four-stroke in a sea of two-strokes, so didn't need oil in the fuel or leave a rider smelling of exhaust fumes. It was also astoundingly economical and its manufacturer, SIA-TA (Società Italiana per Applicazioni Tecniche Auto-Aviatorie), could not keep up with demand. Ducati agreed to assist with production, but it was 1948 before it was sold as a complete moped under the Ducati banner. By now

the communists had removed the Ducati family from the picture, but kept the family name. Bologna has long been known as '*la dotta, la grassa, la rossa*' (the doctor, the fat, the red) after the university that brought Ducati to the city, the food and the communism that saw the Ducati family leave. One of the very first 900SS was sent as a gift to Fidel Castro from the chamber of commerce as a

The Ducati 500GP: this early version with bevel two-valve heads. Renato Amaroli added cambelts and 4-valve heads, having prototyped his ideas in 1963 with a Ducati 250.

The idea that Ducati's future would be V-twins was challenged with this prototype 350cc triple that was intended to herald a 500cc four.

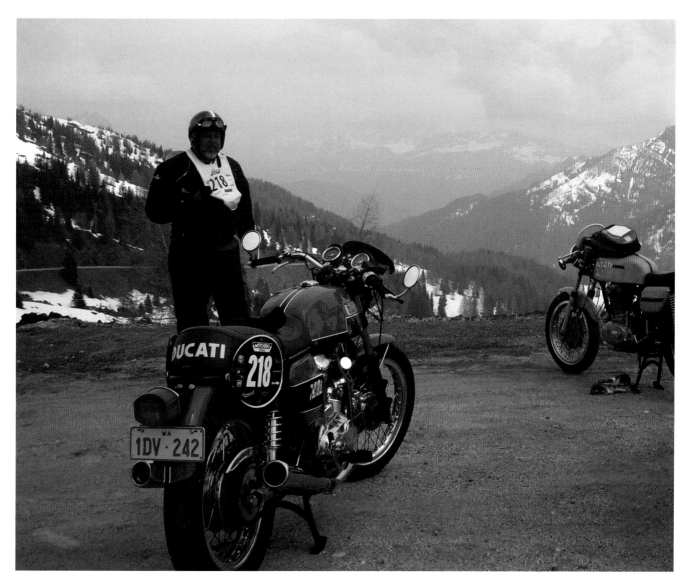

The first production Ducati V-twin was the 750GT, using ideas from the Apollo.

blessing of his ambitions. It is still in a museum in Havana, having only been ridden a few thousand miles.

Before the bevel singles and twins, like the 900SS, Ducati motorcycles had been nothing remarkable – a series of small-capacity, overhead-valve singles – until Fabio Taglioni joined from Mondial in late 1954. He had already experimented with desmodromics at Mondial and was perfectly happy there until he was not invited to the celebrations of Mondial's win at the Milano-Taranto. He simply cleared his desk and left, knowing he had plenty of job offers, not just in the motorcycling world but also at Ford and Ferrari. But Ducati's new chief, Giuseppe Montano, knew what Taglioni craved – the chance to build his own racing motorcycles, free from any interference. He could have earned far more elsewhere, but all the bevel overhead-cam engines, the Pantah range and the TT2 and

1 were one man's vision of how a motorcycle should be. He was occasionally forced into compromises he was unhappy about, but not often. Even when, during the 1970s, Ducati's government paymasters insisted the factory did not go racing, Taglioni simply allowed NCR to claim the credit, including for the 900F1 that Mike Hailwood used to win the 1978 Formula 1 TT. NCR had a small workshop that prepared motorcycles for racing, but they did not have the capacity to manufacture engines.

Taglioni, however, did not believe in 4-valve heads or liquid cooling. It fell to Massimo Bordi to move Ducati into this arena, especially after Cagiva bought Ducati (as detailed in that entry). Although we are comfortable today to think of the Paso, 916 and Monster as Ducati's, they were originally designed as Cagiva's, as the small elephant logos on many components tells. Massimo Bordi was arguably the last Ducati engineer to think radically, embracing the idea of 4-valve desmodromic heads – with Taglioni's help – for his degree thesis. Not many people realize it is he, not Ducati, who holds many of the patents for the design. Bordi was also the brains behind the Supermono and envisaged a Monster-style version with automatic transmission when giant scooters and Honda's DVT gearboxes were still unheard of. For his troubles he was forced out of Ducati and ultimately MV Agusta as well. The modern motorcycle manufacturer prefers

This is a replica of Mike Hailwood's 1978 F1 TT winning bike. It was, in fact, a special order model, available to anyone who could afford it. Based on the old round case racers, it was designated NCR to hide Taglioni's spending on racing rather than because NCR had much, if anything, to do with building these bikes.

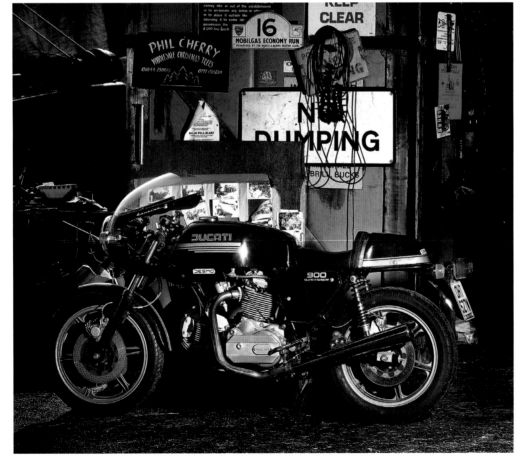

The 900SS was only put into production in 1975 to retrospectively homologate a Castrol Six Hour race winner. The Australian market was Ducati's' biggest for many years, so the run was justified. It came as a shock to Ducati when the 900SS outsold the 860GT by a huge margin, and it became a regular production model.

The Darmah was another model that Ducati had high hopes for, and press reviews were very positive. But sports riders preferred the much lighter and more powerful 900SS, while people wanting a more laid-back motorcycle stuck with the Japanese.

The 600cc TT2, and the later 750cc TT1, were the motorcycles that Taglioni intended his cambelt engine for. Incredibly successful racers, notably in the hands of Tony Rutter; this TT1 was raced by Walter Villa.

The Paso was intended to be a big seller across the world, Tamburini's first styling project post-Bimota. It sold poorly and is probably the best-value classic Ducati you can buy. Early models had an air-cooled 748cc motor; later ones a part liquid-cooled 904cc motor with a six-speed gearbox (hence the 906 designation). The final 907 dropped the Paso name and gained fuel injection and 17in (rather than 16in) wheels. VICKI SMITH/DUCATI.NET

carefully researched projects that are pretty much certain to sell well, rather than one man's vision of what could be.

After Cagiva sold Ducati, only one man deserves singling out as understanding the marque. When Federici Minoli took control in 1996, Ducati was bankrupt and had lost its greatest designers and engineers. But Minoli was not just a turn-around specialist, he was a keen motorcyclist. He understood the love many had for Ducati and their attachment to its history. He used this unique understanding to make Ducati successful and profitable, not just in the showrooms but

The bikes that saved Ducati. The M900 Mostro/Monster was the work of Miguel Galluzzi, who wanted to use an 851 motor from the Desmoquattros, based on his stripped back company bike. Cost, and the need for a big battery, ruled that idea out.

The Monster has become Italy's best-selling motorcycle by some way thanks to endless reinvention. The S4RS here is actually based on the sports touring ST4S, rather than the earlier Monster. EVE PULLEN

The Supermono was incredibly successful in the once popular singe-cylinder racing classes. Another Bordi design, it was in essence a V-twin with the rear cylinder replaced by a balance shaft. This is a version a UK specials' builder had hoped to sell as a small batch rod bike, based on the later V-twins, but the 2008 crash put an end to the project.

also in racing. He understood that super bike racing sold superbikes, but that a MotoGP fan is just as likely to buy a Monster. I met him just once, on a Motogiro recreation (Minoli's idea) in Sicily, where he rode a Multistrada – a motorcycle he launched as much on instinct as anything else – happy to be a motorcyclist for a week. Thanks to him, Ducati is now an incredibly successful business, but very much a design and assembly facility for motorcycles that have only gone into production following extensive market research.

Pierre Terblanche, who styled the Supermono, then came up with the idea of a limited edition evolution of the original Mike Hailwood replica and NCR 900F1. Marketed as the MHe it sold well, but Ducati had not asked the Hailwood family for consent to use Mike's, by then trademarked name. Mike's widow, Pauline, generously accepted a donation by Ducati to the Riders for Health charity as compensation.

Buoyed by the success of the MHe, Ducati put what they called the Sport Classic range into production. The first was the Paul Smart tribute seen here, but the subsequent models sold poorly, although they are now seen as collectible.

Only Ducati have been brave enough to make a MotoGP bike road-legal and put it on sale. A remarkable hand-built motorcycle that was £45,000 new and still worth pretty much the same, although plenty ask much higher prices.

ELECT (1914–23)

A Turin brand established by Ladetto, Ubertalli and Cavalchini, which started building a 492cc flat twin in 1920. The cylinders lay fore and aft with 3-valve heads and the gearbox below the rear cylinder. There were also 498cc versions built under the SAR (Società Reggiana Motocicli) banner in Villadossola in the far north of Italy until 1926 with side- and overhead-valve options. From 1924, SAR also offered a model with a 350cc engine by Bradshaw.

ELMECA (1976–78)

Elmeca (Elettro Meccanica Cafasse) produced pumps for fuel-filling stations in Cafasse, north of Milan. Owner, Piero Chiantelassa, was passionate about off-road sport and persuaded Gilera and their owners Piaggio to supply him with their two-stroke engines, following their decision to abandon off-road competition in 1974. In 1976, Elmeca sold some 600 Regolarità and motocross models, but demand dwindled and racing success proved elusive. For 1977, much improved models were offered but, without the hoped-for sales, production ceased the following year.

ELSA (1920–25)

A 75cc two-stroke was designed by Carlo Sorelli and built in Brescia by ELSA (Elettromeccanica Lucini Società Anonima).

ERCOLI & CAVALLONE (1922–23)

Produced motorcycles powered by a 500cc V-twin. Unusually, it was a two-stroke, with the rear cylinder offset to improve cooling.

EXCELSIOR (1905–12)

An intriguing range of motorcycles built in Brescia. They had a clutch in an era when riders were often expected to pedal up to a speed the engine could pull, and telescopic forks. Originally, engines from Bruneau (built in Tours, France) were used and later the Swiss Zedel engine, before Excelsior moved on to produce its own 235cc motors.

FAGGI (1950–53)

Milan-based, using Villiers motors of 125cc and 198cc, with three- or four-speed gearboxes, in motorcycles and light vans.

FAINI (1923–27)

A Lecco workshop that initially built a 98cc two-stroke, later increased to 123cc. Later still, they produced complete motorcycles, ultimately 200cc and 250cc four-strokes. Some Vassenas were sold under the Faini banner (*see* Vassena).

FALCO (1950–53)

Based in Vercelli, between Milan and Turin, they used motors from Fichtel and Sachs (a forerunner of Sachs).

FANTIC MOTOR (1968–)

Formed by Mario Agrati on leaving his family's Agrati Garelli concern, with the sales manager Henry Keppel. Initially, the intention was to build mini-bikes, go-karts and small off-road motorcycles aimed at the US market. Based in Barzago, a dozen miles north of Garelli's home in Arcore, their first serious stab at a motorcycle was the Caballero: it is a Spanish word for gentleman or even knight, but Keppel actually took the name from his preferred brand of cigarettes. The frame was bought in from Verlicchi and the engine a 50cc Minarelli P4 SS. The hope was to sell 500 units – Fantic actually sold 10,000.

A 100cc Caballero followed along with the famous 50cc and 125cc Choppers, one of the latter given by the UK importers to comedian Dick Emery, a keen motorcyclist happy to be seem with his free toy. But these were unique lightweights from a company that had intended to focus on the off-road market. Inevitably, a 125cc Caballero appeared and, by the mid-1970s, Fantic had a competition depart-

Perhaps the very essence of the 1970s: a sports moped cum chopper. A peaky 50cc two-stroke with the sort of laid-back styling more usually associated with Harley-Davidsons.
P. S. PARROT

ment and were selling models for motocross, enduro and ultimately trials. During the 1980s, Fantic won three trials world championships and seven wins at the Scottish Six Days Trial. The range of trials models were from 50cc to 300cc, often equipped with engines developed in-house.

While the off-road Fantics remain, inevitably now powered by liquid-cooled four-strokes, the Caballero name has been revived, Ducati Scrambler style, for a range of flat track and new wave custom models. All are to be assembled in Treviso using near identical cycle parts, available as 125cc, 250cc and 500cc. In the same way that Ducati market the Scrambler, the Caballero name is given more emphasis than any reference to Fantic. The 125cc engine is a Yamaha Minarelli, the 250cc and 500cc are Chinese Zongshe.

FBM (1951–57)

Fabbrica Bolognese Motocicli was a partnership of Franco Morini and Vittorio Minarelli. Their first offering was

a two-stroke 125cc followed by a four-stroke 125cc, while 50cc two-strokes and 175cc four-strokes were built for third parties. The business was dissolved when the partners went on to establish their own engine manufacturing concerns.

FB MONDIAL (1930–)

The Milanese royalty that was the Boselli family had a small business making commercial three-wheelers and servicing GD motorcycles in Bologna. Racing fan Giuseppe persuaded his three brothers that expanding into motorcycle production would allow them to enter the new world championship series to promote their road bikes. So, the Fratelli Boselli (Brothers Boselli) set up FB Mondial in 1948 and engaged Alphonso Drusiani to build them a 125cc racer. Drusiani ignored the dominant two-stroke wisdom to deliver a bevel drive double overhead-cam single, which took the inaugural 125 World

The chain driven overhead cam of the range topping 175 is clearly evident.

Championship in 1949. Two more 125 world championships might have been added to if they hadn't sold MV one of their bikes.

For open-road racing and for sale to the public, Mondial offered a chain-driven, single overhead-cam racer, their 175cc winning the 1954 Motogiro and Milano-Taranto. Mondial also took the first two places in the sport (road bike) class, and the top three in the competition (race bike) class, with victor Remo Venturi's twin-cam 175cc beating 250s and 500s in the process. Mondial would be the only manufacturer to win both these Gran Fondo (big fund, or prize) races.

By now Drusiani had another engineer working with him, Fabio Taglioni, who would go on to make Ducati world famous. Inspired by Mercedes desmo-powered dominance in the car world, Drusiani designed desmodromic valve gear for his racers, although some believe the engine never ran.

Other bikes in the Mondial range were overhead-valve singles or two-strokes, none over 200cc, and they produced only 1,000 or 2,000 bikes a year. This compared to the 10,000 plus both Gilera and MV Agusta were making, and the 30,000 or so built by Moto Guzzi each year. In the face of such disparity, Mondial had to make savings, including making cheaper and less powerful pushrod and two-stroke engines for their road bikes. But the racers remained wonderfully exotic, winning both the 125 and 250 World Championships in 1957. Mondial, along with all the Italian factories, had then agreed to withdraw from racing at the end of that year, although MV famously had a change of heart.

Soichiro Honda was a fan of Mondial, especially their racing motorcycles (he also admired NSU). Having noticed Mondial's success, and withdrawal from racing, he wrote to the brothers in 1958 to ask if he might buy one of their obsolete engines. The relationship went well,

For some, the ultimate FB Mondial roadster: the overhead-cam 175cc. Although there was a 200cc variant with a cylinder head casting that hinted at twin cams, it was in fact an overhead valve.

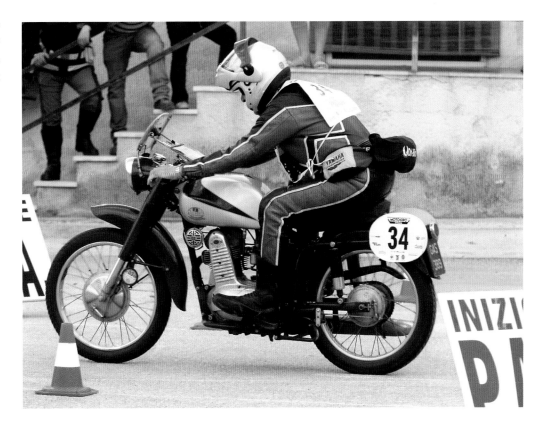

**Another Motogiro
recreation, another
Mondial 175.**
MYKEL NICOLAOU

and a 1956 twin-cam racer duly arrived at Honda's secret camp, developing the RC141 they intended to debut in the 1959 TT. Team leader Kiyoshi Kawashima was
shocked, telling the press years later that 'the Mondial
gave 16.5PS, and our engine just 15.3 – and the Mondial was a three year old design!'. Kawashima had to add
4-valve heads before he could beat the Italian design. The
importance of Mondial's generosity is remembered with
a Mondial 125cc being the first exhibit seen by visitors to
the Honda museum.

In 1961, Count Giuseppe Boselli, still a huge racing
fan, decided long enough had passed since the pact with
Moto Guzzi, Gilera and Benelli that had meant withdrawing from racing. He believed he could put his old
motorcycles back on the track in the hands of Francesco
Villa. This was a low-key return and certainly not backed
with the resources enjoyed during the fifties.

Francesco Villa updated the 125cc twin-cam Mondial
himself, and then managed to take the class win in the
Italian senior championship for three consecutive years.
But Francesco realized that two-strokes were the future,
and set to designing a rotary valve 125cc. In 1964 he debuted the first racing Mondial two-stroke at the Modena
GP, but had to retire when leading, due to a failing con-
denser wire.

In 1965, Francesco again took the national 125cc title on the two-stroke Mondial and immediately penned

a narrower and lighter engine version. Despite Mondial being reluctant to race it under their own name, a
number of the so-called Beccaccino (snipe) were sold to
trusted individuals, including Francesco's brother Walter.
He used it to take the Italian 125 title for Mondial yet
again in 1966 and, unsurprisingly, Mondial were happy
to take the credit. In truth, however, the motorcycle was
really the start of the Villas' own company (see Villa). And
that was really the end of Mondial's racing efforts, and
full-scale manufacture of motorcycles for the road would
soon also cease.

That was almost it, with 1960 seeing the last true
Mondials, even if the factory carried on making engines
until the late seventies. In the interests of economy, the
four-strokes were increasingly replaced by two-strokes
and even a scooter.

Mondial's legacy goes much further than their five riders' and five manufacturers' world championships, and
the Gran Fondo victories. Without Mondial, Fabio Taglioni may not have introduced desmodromics to Ducati,
and Honda may have been humiliated in their early days
of world championship racing and given up.

There was a failed relaunch in 1987 and, in 2003, the
FB Mondial name was revived in Brescia, with the Piega, a 999cc sports bike. It was powered by a Honda SP2
V-twin, the only time Honda has been prepared to allow
another manufacturer to use its engines. There was the

Sammy Miller parading his Mondial 250. He almost won a TT on one, but fell with a seized gearbox at Governor's Bridge, almost in sight of the finishing line. Miller pushed his steed over half a mile, much of it uphill, to finish fifth.

The Mondial Piega, a worthy attempt to re-launch the marque, but ultimately unsuccessful.
MADE IN ITALY MOTORCYCLES

promise of naked versions but the venture failed in 2004. There were attempts to revive the Piega but these came to little or nothing. A further revival came in 2016 with a range of four-stroke 125s built in collaboration with the Boselli family using Piaggio designed and built (in China) engines. A 250cc range is promised.

FERRARI (1952–56)

A small range of two-strokes were built in Milan by the Ferrari brothers, renamed Fratelli Ferrari after the car manufacturer took court action. Unremarkable, apart from the name, the 125cc, 150cc and 160cc engines were very similar to the equivalent Parillas, probably because one of the brothers had worked for them. Not to be con-

fused with Ferraris, also Milan-based, who sold bicycles with Peugeot engines during 1913.

FERT (1926–29)

A range of overhead-cam 175s were built in Milan by Ferruccio Calamida.

FIAMC (1952–53)

The Fabbrica Italiana Auto Moto Cicli was based in Parma and produces a two-stroke 125cc with a two-speed gearbox.

FIAMMA (1935–38)

A Turin-based collaboration between future world champion Nino Farina and Giuseppe Milanaccio. Initially, they just offered an all-alloy, overhead-cam 250cc engine and, later, a complete motorcycle.

FIGINI AND LAZZARI / FIGINI (1898–1910)

Luigi Figini of Milan initially offered engines to bolt on to a bicycle frame's saddle post, and later with a chassis built in-house as the Figini.

FIMER (1952–57)

A 125cc two-stroke scooter and, from 1953, the lightweight Rondine motorcycle with the same engine. Milan again!

FINZI (1922–25)

A circa 600cc (some say 598, others 650) transverse 36-degree V-twin with a three-speed gearbox built in Milan. Also branded Maxima, and based in Voghera, south of Milan.

FIORELLI (1951–62)

Based north of Genoa in Novi Ligure, initially offering 125cc two-strokes and, later, a 175cc. From 1954, re-branded as Motovelo Fiorelli to produce mopeds.

FM (1925–54)

The Milanese Fratelli (brothers) Molteni originally used MAG and Bradshaw engines, but turned to 125cc two-stroke powered scooters and lightweights post-war. Some were branded Molteni.

FOCESI (1948–56)

Alfredo Focesi was a pioneer of Italian cycling in Italy but his Gloria3 M was a moped with a three-speed gearbox. The Gloria 100 had an overhead-valve 98cc engine and four-speed gearbox. A two-stroke 160cc was the final model.

FOCHJ (1954–57)

NSU two-stroke powered lightweights built in Bologna. Later models had NSU 100cc and 250cc four-stoke motors.

FONGRI (1910–30)

A Turin factory founded by Fontana and the Grignani brothers. The first model was a four-stroke vertical single, but Fongri were famous for their longitudinal flat twins. Despite the fact that most of the motorcycles and components were made in-house (or perhaps because of it), records are sparse and contradictory. Complete motorcycles may have not been built until later than 1910, and probably not during the war. A change of premises around 1922 may have been due to Fontana leaving along with, possibly, a Grignani brother. The flat twins were built in mainly *c.*575cc versions, including a water-cooled model. A 500cc competition version was raced by Tazio Nuvolari. Towards the end there were also four-stroke 125cc and 175cc singles.

FORONI (1975–80)

A Modena-based manufacturer of a folding moped with a Franco Morini S5 engine.

FRANCHI (1930–58)

Originally, a spares and accessories business in Milan that, from the early 1950s, offered complete motorcycles with Sachs two-stroke engines. Certainly available as 125cc and 150cc, advertised as Franchi-Sachs, but probably also with *c.*50cc and 100cc motors.

FRECCIA AZZURRA (1951–53)

Stylish sci-fi styled scooter, originally shown with a Puch 125cc motor but sold with a Sachs 150cc two-stroke and four-speed gearbox. Built by Lake Trasimeno for SAI Ambrosini, another aviation business needing to diversify, it quickly ran into trouble at twice the price of Vespas and Lambrettas.

FRERA (1906–36)

La Frera factories were in Tradate near the lakes, and are now a museum mainly dedicated to the motorcycles. One of the largest manufacturers of the period, and an early adopter of a production line, it is well documented with offices in Milan. Indeed, given how many manufacturers are shown as being based in Milan, it is fair to wonder if these were registered offices with manufacture undertaken further afield.

Corrado Frera was born in 1859 in Kreuznach in Germany but was of French origins. He moved to Milan around 1850 and gained Italian citizenship, along with the nickname The German. He started out repairing and upgrading bicycles in the city, but by 1903 he was selling reinforced bicycles with NSU engines to great acclaim.

Swiss Zedel engines were added to the range and, from 1914, produced under licence at Tradate. Frera were the largest supplier of motorcycles to the Italian army during the First World War. By the 1920s, Frera were one of the largest motorcycle manufacturers in Europe, exporting to China and South America – 350cc and 500cc singles were available with side and overhead valves, later joined by a 175cc. In 1922, Corrado Frera was made an Official of the Crown of Italy, the first of awards not just for his motorcycle business, but for the social welfare he offered. Freras won the most important race in Italy, the

ABOVE: This Frera does not even have a gearbox. Early motorcycles often even lacked clutches – engines had sufficient torque to manage without. Note sprocket for pedals, which would be used to get moving and deal with hills: manufacturer's talked of 'LPA' (light pedal assistance) might sometime be needed to keep an engine running.
DAVID BROWN

LEFT: Frera was once hugely successful. Note exposed pushrods and side-valve layout and hand-change gearbox.

Milano-Taranto in 1923 and 1925 and in 1928 total production passed the 50,000 mark.

V-twins of up to 1140cc followed, as did 4-valve heads for the singles. But a recession starting in 1929, combined with the loss of state orders, led to bankruptcy in 1933 and finally closure. There were inevitably attempts to relaunch post-war, unconnected to the Frera family, but none were successful.

FMT (1928–30)

Treviso-based, FMT (Fratelli Mattarello di Treviso) built 132cc two-strokes with either a two- or three-speed gearbox. There was a pressed steel frame model intended for priests.

FRIGERIO (1969–88)

The Frigerio brothers of Treviglio, east of Milan, offered lightweight motorcycles and carts, from 175cc to 350cc, powered by Gilera four-stroke singles.

FUSI (1932–57)

Achille Fusi was originally the FN importer, based in Milan but, following the 1929 economic crisis, he saw a market for a much cheaper motorcycle. Originally called the Ras (after Ethiopian chieftains, to associate it with Italy's ambitions in Africa), Fusi used JAP engines from 175cc to 490cc. Gearboxes were Burman-style, built by Fiat. When Fusi died in 1932 his name was adopted by the factory manager Luigi Beauxfor for JAP-engined 250 and 500s. From 1935, there were in-house designed and built overhead-cam and overhead-valve 250s. A 500cc overhead-valve variant followed and the JAP engines were now built under licence. The purchase of CF brought in a more advanced 250cc in various specifications, including inclined and vertical cylinder versions. From 1950, a Garelli Mosquito-powered moped was added to the range of 250s.

Advertising was nearly always like this: simple line drawings, specifications and performance claims. The 500cc had overhead valves, the 250cc side valves.

FVL (1925–35)

Francesco Vincenzo Lanfranchi (hence FVL) had been a successful racer, the first to average over 120km/h (75mph) in a race. He was born in Florence, raced mainly in France but moved to Milan to start his motorcycle workshop. Initially, he used Swiss 175cc four-stroke Moser engines, but was soon building his own overhead-valve 125cc and 175cc with unit two-speed gearboxes. Eventually, there was also an overhead-cam 175cc with three- and later four-speed gearboxes.

GA (1925–27)

Built by Brevetti Azzara in Milan using a 700cc Blackburne engine and Burman gearbox.

GABBIANO – *SEE* MOTOTECNICA DELL'ITALIA CENTRALE

GABOR (1977)

A 75cc two-stroke enduro motorcycle was built in Dueville near Vicenza. Gabor took third and fourth place in the Italian Six-Day Trial of 1977 but it was not enough to allow mass production.

GAIA (1922–32)

Turin-based Giuseppe Gaia was another bicycle-maker trying his luck with motorcycle manufacture. Initially, he used the German engine Alba, a single-cylinder 192cc side-valve with a non-unit two-speed gearbox. Later models used an astonishing array of different engines, including from DKW, Train, Ladetto & Blatto and Moser. Eventually, he established a factory in Rocca Canavese, north of Turin, to build his own side-valve 175cc with three-speed gearbox.

GALBAI (1921–25)

A range of two-stroke motorcycles were built in Tradate, south-west of Lake Como. First, there was a 276cc single, joined by versions of around 350cc, including a racer. A 500cc V-twin was also offered.

GALBUSERA (1932–55)

Plinio Galbusera first produced motorcycles equipped with Rudge Python engines ranging from 175cc to 500 cc. At the 1938 Milan Show, Adolfo Marama-Toyo-designed two-strokes were shown, a supercharged 250cc V4 and a 500cc V8. Post-war, 125s and 175s were sold initially with Sachs engines and, finally, with Villiers engines.

GALLONI (1920–31)

Founded by Alberto Galloni in Borgomanero, they originally made small, two-strokes. Later, and most impressive, were the 500cc and 750cc side-valve, V-twin cylinders, followed by single-cylinder, four-stroke 250cc to 500cc engines. In 1926, Alfredo Panella became Champion of Italy racing a Galloni, but it was not enough to save the company. The last model was powered by a 175cc Blackburne engine.

GANNA (1923–57)

Motorcycles originally built by Luigi Ganna using side- and overhead-valve 250cc, 350cc and 500cc JAP engines. Later, Python 350cc and 500cc (including the 4-valve) engines and Blackburne 250cc, 350cc and 500cc. In the 1930s, overhead-valve JAP and side-valve Blackburne 175cc were offered. In 1933, Ganna offer their first in-house engine, an overhead-cam 500cc single, eventually joined by 250cc, 350cc and side-valve variants. Post-war production was limited to lightweight two-strokes, using Puch and NSU engines.

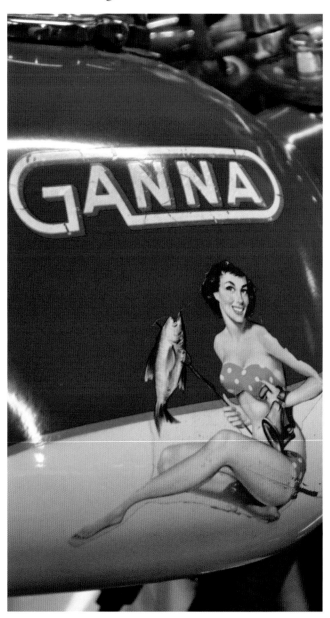

Ganna was famous for their quality of finish and sporting nature. VICKI SMITH/DUCATI.NET

GAOMA (1951–54)

The Gaoma Daino had a purpose-built 63cc two-stroke engine, with a chassis and bodywork by Magni in Milan. A 75cc version followed.

GARABELLO (1903–29)

Francesco Garabello first built a motorcycle using a 240cc single, but soon stretched to 480cc. However, the motorcycle Garabello are famous for is the 1922 984cc longitudinal four. With liquid-cooling, including a radiator with fan, and shaft drive with a universal joint to allow suspension, it was years ahead of its time. It was also far too expensive to sell, and was followed by a 175cc single with shaft drive, liquid cooling and a forward-facing carburettor feeding a rotary valve.

GALIMBERTI (1933–35)

Cesare Galimberti offered modified versions of the Maffeis brothers' motorcycles.

GARANZINI (1922–31)

Brothers Francesco and Orsete Garanzini imported British Verus motorcycles, branding modified 350cc versions as the Veros. Their first eponymous motorcycles used four-stroke JAP and Blackburne engines, successful enough to justify a new factory in 1925 near Milan, and two-stroke Villiers. Subsequently, only the name Garanzini remains and JAP and Blackburne four-stroke engines and two-stroke Villiers of various displacements are mounted. 250cc and 350cc singles built in-house followed, including an overhead-cam version. Records show a c.615cc twin was built, but little evidence of it exists, although a JAP 680cc V-twin powered model was sold.

Francesco Garanzini also sold motorcycles badged as either MFG or MFG with 142cc two-strokes Bekamo motors and 248cc, 348cc and 498cc Blackburne side- and overhead-valve engines and a three-speed transmission.

GARAVAGLIA (1904)

Probably the first dynasphere or monowheel ever shown, a single-wheeled vehicle with the rider within the wheel.

Exhibited at the 1904 Turin Motor Show, with a single-cylinder, four-stroke engine.

GARDINI (1924–25)

Another bicycle factory that moved into motorcycles, based in Forlì, south-east of Bologna. Gardini used DKW two-stroke motors, with both single- and twin-cylinder models. Although the motorcycles lasted barely more than a year, the bicycles survived until 1975.

GARELLI (1912–)

The 1970s Rekord sports moped is the Garelli most people remember, but their greatest motorcycle was probably their first. Aldaberto Garelli designed a 349cc two-stroke, split, single, two pistons working in parallel, and connected a shared gudgeon pin and single conrod. Garelli had perfected his ideas for two-stroke engines at Fiat and, especially, Stucchi before establishing his own factory at Sesto San Giovanni, near Milan.

The remarkable split piston Garelli 350 that, in May 1926, set a speed record of 126mph (203km/h), taking all the class records up to, and including, the 1000cc class. This is the grand prix 350 in its final incarnation. Garelli claimed 20bhp at 4,500rpm and an unfaired top speed of over 80mph (130km/h). Tazio Nuvolari used one and it is said that Carlo Guzzi set his heart on beating the Garelli when he set about designing his first motorcycle. BONHAMS MOTORCYCLES

In its first year, Ettore Girardi gave the 350 Garelli a perfect racing debut by winning the Raid Nord Sud, which would become the Milano-Taranto. Garelli capitalized on this by offering the 'Raid Nord Sud', an over-the-counter production racer, which was used in competition events all over Europe by the great Italian riders of that era, including Tazio Nuvolari and Achille Varzi. World speed records were also set by the factory, the 350cc even taking 1000cc class records.

By 1935, however, motorcycles had been replaced by the production of generators and air compressors but, post-war, Garelli returned with the 1946 Mosquito, a 38cc two-stroke, clip-on engine that could be fitted to a bicycle, later offered as a complete moped.

From 1946 until the 1990s, Garelli made lightweight two-stroke machines, the vast majority mopeds that were astoundingly popular: at one point in the 1950s, Garelli were only outsold by Moto Guzzi in Italy. A 125cc four-stroke was offered between 1959 and 1967, the overhead-valve motor bought in from Parilla. Garelli also made other products such as outboard and go-cart engines. In 1961, they merged with Agrati to become Agrati Garelli.

Garelli's 1980s grand prix machines did justice to their once so innovative split-single, two-strokes of the past, winning the 125 World Championship every year from 1982 to 1987 with Àngel Nieto, Fausto Gresini and Luca Cadalora. Today the name is applied to Chinese-made scooters.

GAZZI (1929–32)

Milan-based and offering 175cc overhead-cam motorcycles, designed and built in-house.

GD/GD GHIRARDI (1923–38)

Bolognese enterprise founded by Mario Ghirardi and Guido Dell'Oglio. Initially, they offered a two-stroke 125cc with a horizontal cylinder, which was used to set speed records, and arced with some success. There are records but no images of an overhead-cam 175cc and a vertical twin 350cc.

GEMS (1921–23)

Galeazzi and Moroni's 268cc two-stroke built in Milan.

GERBI (1952–54)

Asti-based factory using Sachs two-stroke engines and, for mopeds, Eolo.

This is one of two 50cc Garellis that, in November 1963, set eight world records at Monza, including 24h at an average speed of 67.59mph (108.834km/h). This record for a 50cc motorcycle has yet to be broken. BONHAMS MOTORCYCLES

GEROSA (1953–84)

Based in San Polo, near Brescia, they originally produced an overhead-cam 175cc. A 125cc with a two-stroke FBM motor followed, but Gerosa soon come to rely on 49cc Minarelli engines.

GG (1928–34)

Padua-based, west of Venice, and founded by Ugo Gasparetti and Albano Ghisellini, they produced 75cc, 100cc and 125cc two-strokes.

GHEZZI & BRIAN (1995–)

Giuseppe Ghezzi and Bruno (Brian) Saturno's Missaglia workshop, between Monza and the Moto Guzzi factory that supplies the basis for their bikes. The original aim was a Moto Guzzi-powered racer for the Italian Super Twin series. The prototype dominated the 1996 championship, winning nine of the thirty-two races it entered. The follow-up was the Ghezzi and Brian Super Twin 1100, designed to give road riders a replica for the road. In 2002, they were invited by Moto Guzzi to develop what would become the MGS-01. They still offer complete Moto Guzzi-based models, alongside upgrade kits.

The Moto Guzzi MGS-01 was actually designed and prototyped by Ghezzi Brian. These were very much intended as racing motorcycles and, although Moto Guzzi promised it, a road-going version never materialized.
MYKEL NICOLAOU

A pure and simple Ghezzi Brian, with the unique Moto Guzzi Griso hiding behind.

GIACOMASSO (1930–35)

Felice Giacomasso's Turin factory used to manufacture engines. Della Ferrera engines were used initially, followed by Giacomasso's own overhead-cam 175cc and 250cc, while 500cc and 600cc parallel twins followed.

GIANOGLIO (1930–35)

Asti-based factory offering 175cc and 250cc four-strokes. There is also mention of a 75cc two-stroke.

GILERA (1909–)

Founded by Giuseppe Gilera, with a factory in the grounds of the family villa in Arcore, close to Milan. Initially, they produced side- and overhead-valve singles, the first of which was the VT 317, and later overhead-cam racing 500cc singles. Gilera became one of the biggest motorcycle manufacturers in Italy – in the world, in fact, with a second factory in Argentina. Between the wars, Gilera were one of the Big Three Italian motorcycle man-

Quite possibly Mr Gilera himself on one of the early motorcycles, circa 1910. PIAGGIO/GILERA

ufacturers, along with Bianchi and Moto Guzzi. After the Second World War, Guzzi became the clear market leader building up to 30,000 bikes a year, but Gilera and newcomer MV Agusta could still manage sales in excess of 10,000 motorcycles a year.

Gilera had decided to focus on big bikes, especially the Saturno 500, which had first raced in 1940. Gilera had built many 500cc singles for the military during the war and sought to build on their expertise to see off the many newcomers to the lightweight motorcycle market. They followed the Saturno up with the brilliantly received B300, which doubled up their pushrod 150cc single to produce what should have been a highly profitable 305cc twin. But even the modest B300 was too expensive to buy and run in 1950s Italy, and sales were disappointing. The market wanted sporting 175s and by the time Gilera launched their 175 Sport in 1956, the competition had pulled out significant leads in terms of product and racing success; the future lay with newcomers like Ducati and Laverda.

Gilera briefly flirted with a pushrod 172.5cc Sferica (hemispherical) to race in the Motogiro, focusing on the 500cc class in the Milano-Taranto. These Sfericas had the hemispheric cylinder-head design of Gilera's all-conquering 500cc four grand prix (and Milano-Taranto) racer. They were listed and entered in races as 150 Sports because that was what Gilera had in the showrooms. The results for the basic 150cc had been promising: Vezzalini managed class wins and fourth overall in the 1955 Giro, the first non-Morini home (this was the year Mendogni won on the controversial overhead cam Rebello) and finished just ahead of Degli Antoni on Taglioni's new bevel-driven, overhead-cam Marianna. Despite such heady competition, Gileras took five of the top ten places. Even so, the engineers in Gilera's Arcore workshops must have realized something special would be needed for the 1956 Giro, and started penning the Sferica. But it was no match for the rapidly improving competition, which was pushing the rulebook to the limit in a way Gilera did not.

Gilera had assumed the marketplace would remain as it had been pre-war, with many manufacturers offering lightweights that were only profitable if sold cheaply and in large numbers. The real money had been made selling 500cc singles to wealthy enthusiasts, and Gilera believed the Saturno to be superior to the equivalent Bianchi and Moto Guzzi. Like those bikes, the Saturno's value today still seems to depend on an Italian buyer, and if sterling's stronger than the euro, you can pick them up for less than the price of a Ducati 175. Some might say that's fair, the baby Ducati showing off classy cycle parts and a bevel-driven, overhead-cam against the Gilera's more prosa-

Gilera 500cc side-valve single. DAVID BROWN

A rather beautiful and original motorcycle, despite packing just 50cc. KLAUS NAHR

The glorious Saturno. This is a 1947 model. MARCELLO

The replica Gilera 500cc four is warmed up for a parade at Sammy Miller's museum.

ic chassis and simple pushrod engine. But dust down the history books and you get a different story. The Saturno was the replacement for the Otto Bulloni (8-bolt), which in turn replaced the Quattro Bulloni (4-bolt), the names referring to the fixings of the barrel to the crankcases. Ettore Villa had ridden an Otto Bulloni to victory in the 1939 Milano-Taranto, beating off the works Bianchis.

The first few Saturnos were built in 1940, and Massimo Masserini took one to victory in the Targa Florio, the final time bikes competed in the Sicilian event. The production Saturno Sport also won the final Milano-Taranto in 1956, when Pietro Carissoni piloted it to a surprise win. Even on closed circuits, the Gilera could occasionally beat its famous 4-cylinder sibling. Unlike the Gilera grand prix four, the Saturno was designed in-house, influenced by a long line of 498.7cc Gilera singles. The obvious competitor in Britain was the BSA Gold Star, lighter but less cleverly engineered than the Italian bike.

The gap between even the basic Turismo Saturno and the Sport was little more than furnishing the Sport with an alloy head and barrel: even the Competizione version only gained different valves, camshaft, carburettor (a 35mm Dell'Orto), piston and gear rations. This meant that racers suffered from valve train wear, a side-effect of the 19bhp Turismo's marginal lubrication system being identical across the range. The difference in the running gear was even less, limited to different tyres and colours. All models initially shared the same girder forks and

The Gilera B300 was in essence two of the firm's 150cc singles. Another poor seller, it was part of Gilera's post-war decline.

The B300 again, but note the Ducati Mike Hailwood Replica: it is one of the last with the 'Mille' (1000) engine. Behind it is a MotoBi.

Detail of the Gilera racing four. Contrast this to the image overleaf.

Gilera's parallelogram rear suspension that dated from 1935. The factory racers of 1947 debuted blade girder forks with a full-width front drum and engine tweaks, including a 35mm SS carb that pumped output up to 35bhp. Winning first time out at the San Remo circuit, the press immediately dubbed the evolving racer 'Sanremo', a name the factory were happy to adopt for future Competiziones. A Sanremo was the first Gilera on the TT's mountain course, a substitution for the 500cc four that Australian Tony McAlpine had asked to race in 1951.

The original Saturno was designed by Giuseppe Salmaggi who joined Gilera from Saolea who, along with FN, were then one of Belgium's main motorcycle manufacturers. It was immediately competitive against the Moto Guzzi Condor, although it's doubtful that more than five Saturnos were built before war brought production to a halt. Post-war, the racing Saturnos winning were helped by only poor-quality fuel being available and the ban on supercharging. Some privateers managed to address the Saturno's pre-war layout, updated with twin overhead-cam cylinder heads and replacing the oddball rear suspension with a conventional layout using Fiat Topolino shock absorbers. Although the factory only built a few works bialbero (twin cams), for 1951, production models gained telescopic forks, but for one year only kept Gilera's patented rear suspension: the model was dubbed the 'Little Bastard,' and conventional rear suspension followed.

The Sanremo racer with conventional suspension was christened the Piuma (feather), despite weight actually increasing over the Sanremo. It has been suggested that the name was a backhanded compliment to Norton's featherbed frame, but the two designs were very different, and the Gilera's notably inferior. Even so, the Piuma's conventional tubes were an improvement over its predecessor, aided by in-house telescopic forks and Sturcher rear suspension units. Developed over the winter of 1950/51, Luigi Gilera (founder Giuseppe's brother) seconded Franco Passoni, from his position as number two to Sandro Colombo in the grand prix team, to develop the Sanremo into the Piuma. He specified a bigger sump and barrel finning, and a 7:1 compression ratio helped deliver 38bhp at 6,000rpm. Success was immediate, with a win in the debut race at Voghera, and production racers (from 1953) were successful all over the world, especially in South America, an important facet for Gilera's Argentine factory. By 1955, Gilera were claiming 42bhp for the Piuma and, although the official records show a 500 Sport won the final Milano-Taranto in 1956, Gilera expert Raymond Ainscoe thinks it was a Piuma.

In truth, Sports were often upgraded to Piuma spec, right through to the mid-sixties, when the bike was still a competitive privateers' mount. With conventional suspension, a Piuma is much easier to copy than the blade-forked Sanremo, whether you're trying to build a club-

man's racer or sting a buyer – something to bear in mind if you're lucky enough to be looking at one. Unlike the Sanremo, the Piuma was never run in grand prix against the fours, possibly because Geoff Duke had resolved the multis' handling and Gilera's fortunes were in decline. Not only had the factory failed to address the lightweight home market, it had little overseas representation and exports were never seen as a priority. The factory was more than happy to join Guzzi's and Mondial's pact to withdraw from racing in 1957. But privateers continued racing the Saturno, helped, as in all its incarnations, by fantastic versatility. The 500cc pushrod single excelled as a tourer and police motorcycle (the police bikes have an ultra-low first gear), but the Saturno made an effective competition tool, off-road as well as on-track, and excelled as a fast road bike.

If Gilera meant the Saturno to cuckold the previously dominant Bianchis and Guzzi Condor, they were more than successful. And it didn't stop there: Saturno sidecars (including a 582cc factory racer) won every national Swiss and Italian event in 1946 and 1947, and were still capable of victories up until 1970. Last, but not least, there were the off-road bikes. Ettore Villa had first entered a motocross race outside his native Rome on a Saturno after converting it to a rigid rear-end late in 1948. From then until 1960, the Saturno was available in motocross spec, Gilera embracing the sport at all levels. With the off-roaders differing from the road racers in little more than running gear and carburettors sizes, the Saturno had proved competitive in every aspect of motorcycle sport, emphasizing the point by winning four French and four Italian off-road titles. In the end, around 6,000 Saturnos were built, mainly between 1946 and 1954, although there was a final run in 1959 for the military. 1947 saw over a thousand roll out of the factory, but even that was nothing compared to the sales of other manufacturers' lightweights and scooters. The Second World War had changed the motorcycle market beyond recognition.

But it is the racing fours that dominate Gilera's history, and are closely linked to the MV Agustas they competed against. Gilera was convinced that victory in the new 500 World Championship would be the ultimate advertising campaign, and was happy to buy in the OPRA Rodine in-line four, despite the fact the design could trace its roots back almost thirty years.

In the early 1920s, Carlo Gianni and Piero Remor, funded by Count Bonmartini, started to develop the idea of a 500cc four, which they believed was the perfect compromise for a racing engine. The first prototypes were referred to as a GRB (Gianini, Remor, Bonmartini).

Around 1929, Piero Taruffi was recruited as a test

Period Gilera factory publicity shot of a side-valve single. It is almost impossible to believe that this, and the racing 500cc four, came from the same factory. PIAGGIO/GILERA

ABOVE: **Rare Sferica 175, built for competition. The standard 150cc model had pushrods that ran vertically to parallel valves in an almost flat combustion chamber. This Sferica has a hemispherical combustion chamber, valves set at 45 degrees to one another, operated by pushrods that cross over each other.**

ABOVE: **Publicity shot for the 150cc Arcore, the last four-stroke in Gilera's range.** PIAGGIO/ GILERA

RIGHT: **The Arcore (named after the town the Gilera factory was in) was a very pleasant ride, but the styling was not popular.** MICK

rider. Bonmartini renamed the four after another of his companies, OPRA (Officine di Precisione Romane Automobilistiche) and entered it into the Grand Prix of Rome. Ridden by Umberto Faraglia, the OPRA briefly led until the engine failed. Taruffi, initially disappointed to have been passed over, won on his Norton.

Development brought water-cooling and supercharging, and a much improved chassis. Six of these versions were built, known as the Rondine (swallow). Taruffi and Amilcare Rossetti raced two of these in the prestigious Grand Prix of Tripoli, taking first and second place after a hard race against Omobono Tenni aboard his Moto Guzzi Bicilindrica.

Bonmartini placed ownership of the Rondine project into another of his companies, Compagnia Nazionale Aeronautica, which is why there are occasional references to a CNA Rondine. In 1934, Bonmartini sold CNA to the aircraft manufacturer Caproni in Milan, who had no interest in the Rondine. Taruffi approached Giuseppe Gilera who immediately bought everything associated with the project, convinced it was the basis of a fine racing machine. By 1936, the four was making 60bhp, an astonishing output for the era.

Post-war, with supercharging banned, Remor revisited the project with features from his later 250cc four and adopted, most obviously, a return to air cooling. This gave Gilera five 500 World Championships on the trot from 1950, with a brace of titles for Umberto Masetti, a hat trick for Geoff Duke and the 1957 title for Libero Liberati. There was also a win in the Milano-Taranto for Bruno Francisci, who simply ditched the battery powered lights at daybreak on his way to setting the race's fasted ever time.

In 1969, the company was bought by the Piaggio and a range of lightweight two-strokes followed. In 1985, a new 350cc twin-cam, single engine, later stretched to 558cc, was originally intended for dual-purpose motorcycles but also powered a new Saturno and racing Piuma. These were fascinating and enjoyable motorcycles, with a huge following in Japan. However, sales in much of the rest of the world during this era were of far more powerful, usually – with great irony – Japanese motorcycles, and Gilera's new singles struggled to find a home.

Gilera's most interesting motorcycle in its final years was surely the CX125, with single swing arms front and rear. First shown in 1989, the Gilera CX finally reached production in 1991, and was sold until the Arcore factory's closure in 1993, with approximately a thousand built. The aerodynamic bodywork (the CX name hinted at a low coefficient of drag) also added to the futuristic look of the bike. The 125cc two-stroke made about 30bhp and propelled the CX to a claimed top speed of over 100mph (160km/h) – a bold claim intended to emphasize the aerodynamic effectiveness of the fairing.

Another publicity shot – during the 1970s and 1980s, Gilera turned to off-road competition in the hope of improving sales. PIAGGIO/GILERA

The 1981 factory Gilera 250 Competizione. Fernando Muñoz achieved second place in the 250 Spanish Championship. PEPROVIRA

The new Saturno had an engine designed and built by Gilera, aimed at the Japanese market.

Luciano Marabese is credited with the design, whose previous creations include the Bimota DB1. Sadly, the little Gilera sold poorly; Italian teenagers wanted race-replicas, and the roomy Gilera was more sports-tourer with a high price reflecting the high-tech chassis.

In 1993, Piaggio closed the Arcore factory and Gilera effectively became a scooter and commuter brand. However, in 2008, the Aprilia RSA250 that had won the two previous 250 World Championships with Jorge Lorenzo was rebranded as a Gilera to commemorate the marques centenary. Marco Simoncelli rode it to Gilera's final world championship.

To celebrate the anniversary of Bob McIntyre setting the first 100mph lap of the TT course at the 2018 Classic TT, Michel Dunlop rode this replica. He – of course – averaged just over 100mph.

The last Gilera to win a world championship – the RSA 250. Ridden by Marco Simoncelli, it was basically a rebranded Aprilia to commemorate Gilera's centenary.

THESUPERMAT

Gilera's CX was one its final models, unpopular at the time but now very collectable.

GIRARDENGO (1951–54)

Motorcycle factory founded in Alessandria by famous cycling champion Costante Girardengo, producing 125cc and 175cc two-strokes.

GITAN (1950–85)

Gino Tansini (hence Gi-Tan) initially used engines from Mi-Val, offering a two-stroke 125cc and an overhead valve 160cc (later 175cc) singles from a factory in Caorso, south-east of Milan. Gitan briefly fitted their own engines, before focusing on mopeds from the 1960s on.

GIULIETTA – *SEE* PERIPOLI

GN (1920–25)

Motorcycles built in Turin by Giuseppe Navone – one of his many brands. He absorbed Baudo in 1929, offered Navone-branded models the same year and Itala-badged motorcycles from 1933 to 1939. All used imported engines in a wide variety of capacities – the earlier models the French Chaise, Train and, possibly, Villiers power plants. Python motors were used for Itala.

GORI (1969–83)

Giancarlo Gori, along with a cofounder of SWM (Speedy Working Motors), initially produced children's motor-

cycles but had great success with a 125 Sachs engined six-speeded sportster in hill climbs. Gradually they became entirely off-road oriented, switching from Sachs to Rotax engines, and effectively became an offshoot of SWM.

GR (1924–27)

Count Gino Revelli (hence GR) imported Henderson motorcycles into Italy, and his brother Mario won the 1925 Monza Grand Prix aboard a JAP 500cc single in a chassis Gino had designed. Subsequently, road-going versions were made available.

GUAZZONI (1935–77)

Founded in Milan by Aldo Guazzoni, initially they built engines for others. Post-war they manufactured a 150cc two-stroke for FBM and then, like many other small factories, focused on sports mopeds. Many had the exhaust exiting the rear of the cylinder, which became something of a Guazzoni trade mark.

GUIA (1950–54)

Milan-built, two-stroke 125s.

GUIZZARDI (1926–33)

Adelmo Guizzardi manufactured 125cc and 175cc four-strokes in Turin.

HRD (1980–87)

No link to the British company of the same name, HRD (Happy Red Devils!) was founded in Busto Arsizio, near Varese, by designer Luciano Marabese. Using TAU 125cc

motors, a range of competition bikes was initially offered followed by fully faired road bikes. Some called them mini Bimotas, as much for the high prices as for the innovation. Merged with Kram-It in 1987.

IBIS (1925–29)

Turin-based factory, mainly producing mopeds but also a 175cc two-stroke.

IDROFLEX (1949–54)

Launched with a 105cc horizontal cylinder, two-stoke motorcycle, with 125cc versions following; also mopeds. All built in Milan.

IMN (1952–58)

Industria Meccanica Napoletana started with a Garelli Mosquito-powered moped and a 100cc overhead-valve motorcycle, the Baio. Two-strokes of 50cc to 75cc followed, including a scooter, but most intriguing is the Rocket 200. Shown at the end of 1956, this featured a 200cc overhead-valve with shaft drive.

INNOCENTI – *SEE* LAMBRETTA

ISO (1948–66)

Known as a factory of refrigerators and accessories for the railways, Isothermos bought the rights of the Ferretto scooter, introducing it in 1950 as a modified version with a two-stroke engine with a split cylinder of 123cc, followed by a second one with separate lubrication and shaft transmission. The engine was also used for the Isetta, later built under license by BMW. In 1961, a series of 125cc and 175cc motorcycles appeared; two years later, Iso switched to the production of luxury cars.

ITALA – *SEE* GN

ITALEMMEZETA – *SEE* ITALJET

ITALJET (1961–2003)

Leopoldo Tartarini's factory in San Lazzaro di Savena near Bologna should be more famous than it is. Tartarini styled three of the exhibits in the Art of the Motorcycle collection– a unique achievement. He was offered a ride with MV

Clymer, famous for its workshop manuals in the US, bought the rights to the Indian name and commissioned Italjet to build a new range using British engines. This one used the Velocette 500.

Agusta but turned it down to focus on the family motorcycle dealership. Even so, he won the 1952 Milano-Taranto sidecar class and the inaugural Motogiro outright. He used his racing connections to source 125cc MZ engines, selling complete bikes as Italemmezeta (Italia MZ). Next was a Minarelli-engined sports moped, the first motorcycle to wear the Italjet name. The next significant model was the Grifon with a Triumph 650 engine. This became Floyd Clymer's Indian with a Royal Enfield Interceptor motor, and Clymer also had Italjet build Velocette-powered Indian 500s. This led to building a version of the Laverda 750, sold in the US as the American Eagle.

Italjet almost always bought engines in, and the 350cc four stoke single they used was reputedly built by Ducati. Italjet had close ties to that factory, including Tartarini styling the Ducati singles from the final Mark III on, the early V-twins and helping with designing and building the later parallel twins and the Darmah.

Italjet's greatest commercial success was probably the hub centre steered Dragster scooter, but when the scooter market collapsed (*see* Aprilia), Italjet went with it. The Hinckley Triumph-powered triples that had been planned to power a new Italjet Grifon, never went into production.

ITALMOTO – *SEE* MASERATI

ITOM (1944–68)

Industria Torinese Meccanica built single-cylinder two-strokes of between 49cc and 65cc, the most famous being the Astor. There were also Zundap and Minarelli 125s, built in small numbers. But it is the competition 50s that were successful out of all relation to Itom's size. Sergio Bongiovanni won the 1966 Italian championship aboard one, and others who raced them included Mike Hailwood, Bill Ivy and Dave Simmonds. The 50cc class of the 1961 French Grand Prix was won by Jean-Claude Serre on an Itom, although it would not be recognized

Itom was most famous for its racers.

as a world championship class until the following year. Beryl Swain rode an Itom as the first woman to compete in (and finish) an Isle of Man TT in 1962, by then a 50cc world championship round.

JONGHI (1930–57)

Alessandro Nagas and Tullio Ray built an overhead-valve 350cc in Milan from 1925 to 1928, sold as the Nagas & Ray. Dealings with creditors meant the model was relaunched in 1930 under the Jonghi banner, a French–Italian concern. 100cc and 125cc two-strokes, alongside a 125cc four-stroke, survived the war when a new range of 250cc two-stroke singles were sold from the early fifties. These were mainly for the French market, but like so many other factories, the arrival of cheap cars heralded the end of the marque.

JUNIOR (1924–36)

A range of two-strokes built near Livorno: initially a 350cc single, a 250cc and 125cc were later built. It was also possible to specify an imported engine, notably the Blackburne 350cc. The factory folded when the owner died in Ethiopia.

KOSMOS (1976–84)

Based in Liscate, east of Milan, and best known for two-stroke off-road motorcycles of 80cc, 250cc, 350cc and 480cc. There were also 80cc and 125cc road versions.

KRAM-IT (1970–89)

Based in Arcore, building two-stroke off-road motorcycles with 50cc and 80cc Minarelli engines, and larger models with Rotax engines. Merged with HRD in 1987, and there are mentions of the later name being used on a Yamaha-powered motorcycle, but no trace of either after 1989.

LADETTO & BLATTO (1927–32)

Emilio and Giovanni Ladetto and designer Angelo Blatto originally offered two- and four-stroke motorcycles from 132cc to 247cc. A side-valve 250cc and overhead-valve 175cc followed. In 1930, Blatto retired and his name was dropped from the Turin factory's subsequent production.

L'ALBA (1924–26)

Milan-based Giorgio Valeri built motorcycles with German overhead-valve, 198cc engines.

LAMBRETTA (1947–72)

Although Lambretta is rightly thought of as Innoceti's scooter brand, rather than associated with motorcycles, it made at least one of the latter. Originally shown at the 1951 Milan Show with a dry-sumped, overhead-cam engine, the Lambretta 250GP had gained a wet sump and twin-cam heads by the time it was retired in 1953. One bike (the first of two built) was discovered abandoned under a pile of rubbish when the Lambretta factory closed in 1972. The bike was designed by Giuseppe Salmaggi and raced, not particularly successfully, by Romolo Ferri and Cirillo Pagani. The 54 × 54mm square engine used shaft final drive and markedly resembles the later Moto Guzzi layout.

Lambretta set many speed records, usually on autostrada closed for their attempts.

Those who worked on the bike say it was almost impossible to get the engine running well – on one occasion, despite working all night, the factory had to abandon a race at Misano. From then on it was relegated to publicity shots before being forgotten. Brand owners Innocenti focused on building Lambretta's image, including a 1967 calendar project with Jean Shrimpton, to no avail. The factory moved pretty much lock, stock and barrel from Milan to India, to make copycat bikes for Scooter India Ltd, although the Lambretta name stayed in Italy and now rests with Fiat.

LAMPO (1925–30)

A Turin factory building sporting two-strokes of 123cc, 173cc, 198cc and 247cc. There was also a 173cc overhead-valve engine. Engines were bought in from Piazza. The factory closed in 1926, but was relaunched in 1930 by former employee, Mario Sporeni, to offer the 175s again, albeit briefly.

LARDORI (1924–27)

A factory in Castellina in Chianti, building motorcycles with French 350cc Train engines and an Ideal three-speed gearbox.

LAURENTI (1955–)

Based in Bologna, Edmondo Laurenti and son offer an overhead-cam 175cc.

LAVERDA (1949–)

Another factory that diversified into small motorcycle production after the Second World War, but Laverda were not being forced to give up manufacturing military equipment. The family had been making agricultural machinery since 1873, and were keen for any opportunity to add another string to the factory's bow. Commuter motorcycles were seized on by Francesco Laverda when looking for chances to diversify. Assisted by engineer Luciano Zen, he started work in 1947 on an innovative four-stroke 75cc machine.

Laverda's reputation for building tough, reliable bikes was built on the success of their lightweight machines in the Italian long-distance classics. In the 1953 Milano-Taranto, the company's 'Tarantina' (Little Taranto) model filled the first fourteen places in the 75cc class, remarkable for a manufacturer that had only been in full production for three years. Laverda's advertising was headlined '*L'utilitaria che vince le corse!*' – colloquially 'The commuter that wins races!'.

The ensuing Laverda sales' boom during the mid-fifties

ABOVE: **For many marque fans, the Jota defines Laverda.**

Laverda's 75cc and 98cc singles were both reliable and fast.

saw 38,000 of the 75cc and its 98cc sibling pass through the showrooms, making them one of the most commercially successful Italian motorcycles of the 1950s. Alongside other lightweight singles, in 1961 a 200cc overhead-valve, parallel twin was launched with the gear change on the left-hand side – the opposite of the European convention. American riders, however, were more used to this arrangement, which showed what Francesco Laverda and his son, Massimo, were thinking. Massimo had been sent to the US to study and research what American buyers liked. The answer was big British twins, despite their occasional unreliability, and the new Honda CB77 Super Hawk. The latter may have only displaced 305cc, but it quickly gained a reputation as a fine sporting motorcycle with perfect reliability.

Laverda and Moto Guzzi were the first Italian manufacturers to realize that cheap cars, such as the Fiat 500, Citroen 2CV and the Austin Mini, would spell the end of the motorcycle industry if they could not expand into the leisure market, rather than pander to those who simply needed transport. Massimo Laverda was brave enough to accept he had limited resources, and a methodical, rather than inspirational, engineer in Luciano Zen. So Massimo bought a Honda CB77, as well as a Norton 650SS that he admired for its featherbed frame and a BMW69S, which he recognized as a highly competent all-rounder. With Zen he stripped all three to their core before sitting down together at the drawing board.

The resulting Laverda 650 was massively over-engineered and weighed 25 per cent more than a Triumph Bonneville, but this would garner reliability and also help minimize vibration. However, the alloy castings were superb, especially the deliberately close-finned cylinder barrels. Oddly, for a motorcycle aimed at the US market, it had a right-hand gearshift.

The sturdy engine meant it could take a big increase in power, and almost immediately the 650cc was enlarged to 744cc. Laverda magnificently turned this into a beautiful sports bike with the 1971 SFC (Super Freni Competizione) or super brakes competition. Genuinely hand-built, and initially only sold to cherry-picked customers, less than 600 were made by the time production ended with the alloy-wheeled 1976 bikes. The SFC was always outrageously expensive, but the factory claimed to test every SFC to be sure it made at least 70bhp, at a time when a Honda 750 struggled to make much more than a genuine fifty. It was highly successful in endurance racing – the reason it was painted orange. Yellow is the easiest colour to see in the dark, but was already being used by a Honda team, so Laverda painted their racers orange as the next best option. Sadly, however, endurance racing was unknown in Laverda's target US market and was not even yet afforded world championship status. Laverda needed an even faster model that would sell based on road tests alone.

A rare 750 Laverda twin. It was replaced almost immediately with the 750.

The American Eagle was an idea born in the US but built by Laverda.

Laverda did try to diversify. The Chott 250 in the foreground was a good off-roader but could not compete on price with the Japanese.

Laverda's original 1000cc triple hailed from 1969, at a time when 750cc twins were big news, even though it was 1973 before production began in earnest. The triples were designated 3C (3 *cilindri* – cylinders), with the prototype's outboard cam chain moved to the more traditional home between cylinders for production: the engine actually weighed less that the 750s. Numbers built were initially kept low, helping the factory develop the bike's early shaky reliability, and upgrading to front discs on still spoked wheels: early bikes just had two leading shoe front drums on 35mm forks. Laverda started development of the triple for endurance racing in 1972 and competed in the 1974 European Championship. The following year saw Zen's 'Space Frame' – a birdcage-like affair that enclosed the engine – introduced for racing to eliminate the tendency for high-speed weaving that the earlier bikes exhibited. A very large fairing was also fitted to provide better weather protection during 24h races.

By 1975, the 3C was trustworthy and fast enough for production racing success. To build on this, British importer Roger Slater wanted a high-performance version that he could race and charge a premium for, with a name rather more evocative than the factory's suggested 3CL (*leggera* – lighter – celebrating the new alloy wheels). Jota was once just a Spanish gypsy dance, danced in rapid triple time. With Roger Slater's Laverda, the name Jota became a rubric, and history was made.

A Laverda scooter hides behind an RGA, one of the final triples.

The SFC twin was a bare-bones racer on the road and successful endurance racer.

Later Jotas had a new crankshaft layout and a half-fairing.

The new wheels brought triple discs and a fibreglass tailpiece. Roger Slater's specification meant that Jotas were delivered to him without exhaust systems. Roger was far-sighted enough to keep records of the numbers on the bikes as they were uncrated. The original Jotas have no Italian homologation plate because it was not homologated for road use or, by this time, with its right-foot gear shift, US legal. But the Jota really might have been, as engineer and writer Royce Creasey put it, the last of the real motorcycles.

Laverda weren't the first to use the Jota name, being beaten to it when Lamborghini badged a limited run Muira 'Jota'. Massimo Laverda had worked at Ferrari and Maserati, but drove a Lamborghini because he liked the idea that, like Laverda, they had started out making agricultural equipment. But the Italians using the word Jota is odd, because, the Italian alphabet doesn't have a 'J' in it. Italians usually pronounce Jota, *Yoe-ta*.

In the long, hot summer of 1976, the Jota scorched its way into history when *Motor Cycle* declared it the world's fastest road bike – the accolade every manufacturer wanted for their flagship. The big Laverda had tripped the MIRA speed trap at over 140mph (225km/h) with a mean average of 137.8mph (221.7km/h), a figure barely credible at the time. Laverda had been racing the big triples almost from the model's launch and so had developed parts for racing. These included the endurance cam, otherwise known as the 4/C, and some high-compression pistons. Slater's, as the UK importer, were enthusiastically promoting the Laverda brand through their race team. It was inevitable that the factory race kit parts would find their way into their workshop and, as a result, Roger Slater had developed a very rapid 3C, which was being campaigned by rider Pete 'PK' Davies.

Roger had been doing a lot of dynamometer work on the triple, developing a big-bore collector box, which proved critical in unlocking the triple's potential. This collector box, fitted with a set of unrestricted exhausts commissioned from Ariel Square Four restorer Tim Healey (together with the factory cams and pistons), completed the classic Jota specification.

The Jota amassed an impressive competition record, winning the coveted Avon Production Series title in its debut year. The following year (1977) Jotas had a successful showing in the first ever Formula 1 TT. In atrocious weather, Mick Hunt brought home the first Jota in sixth place. Four other Jotas had entered the race and all finished in respectable positions (John Kirkby came ninth). If they had registered for a team prize, Slater's would have won the manufacturer's class. Elsewhere in Europe, the Jota was beginning to make its mark: Lennart Backstrom took the Swedish Super Bike title in 1978 and Davies took the Avon Production Championship in 1978 and 1979.

For 1978, Laverda grew the triple to 1115cc, for the 1200TS and Mirage. For some reason, these never caught the public's imagination, despite being by common consensus nicer than the 1000s to ride. Slater's could even tune them to exceed 150mph (241km/h) and today they probably offer the best-value 1970s models. From 1982, Laverda switched to a 120-degree (from 180) crankshaft they had first experimented with in endurance racing.

The Formula 500 was another model built as a production racer.

Engines were also rubber mounted to try and compete with the smoothness of the Japanese competition.

Most impressive of these new bikes was the RGS, with a new, lower frame and beautiful Bayflex bodywork that extended to a half fairing. A number of variants followed: the RGS1000 Corsa, with an extra 10bhp courtesy of forged high-compression pistons and cylinder head modifications and the RGS1000 Executive, with additional fairing panels and tiny integral panniers. There was also an SFC version aimed at the Italian TT1 championship. But these were outrageously expensive motorcycles that were hardly better than the alternatives, although offering far more style and character. So cheaper, RGA unfaired versions were offered, much improved by the UK importer with a twin headlight Sprint fairing. They also showed a two-stroke 350 V3 in 1985, but, in truth, projects such as this were a dubious use of scarce resources. None of this was enough to find a successful niche and by the late-1980s, Laverda had fallen to the Japanese factories.

How different it had been a decade earlier when success of the 750 twins and 1000 triples convinced Laverda they should broaden their range to compete with the Japanese. The 1977, 497cc, 8-valve Alpina was the result (the name changed to Alpino – and Zeta for the US – when BMW pointed out their tuning arm was called Alpina), joined by a 350cc sibling in the home market. Specification and finish trumped not only the Italian competition, but the Japanese too. The 500cc weighed barely more than the Yamaha RD400, and had an elegant cohesion that made it one of the best-looking bikes of the time. Like the Montjuic, the overall look was the work of Lino Borghesan, a much underrated stylist and frame designer. The rest was down to Laverda stalwarts Luciano Zen and Adriano Valente.

1978 brought the Alpino S with a balancer shaft and revised styling, together with the bare bones Montjuic, a mini Jota dreamed up by UK importer Roger Slater. Most Montjuics feature the F500 close ratio gearbox, as well as over-the-top tuning: *Bike* magazine described the Montjuic as 'best ridden after removing your brain', one reason why so many suffered premature engine failure and now house standard Alpino engines.

But Laverda asked for half as much cash again as their Japanese competitors, and sold barely 5,000 of these twins. The final sales push was the Formula 500, a club racer that became the fastest Laverda ever to lap the Isle of Man. But that was the end for the Laverda family's motorcycling adventure, although we will return to them with the story of the V6 later, for the sake of continuing the story of the middleweight twins.

The right to build Laverda motorcycles finished up with the Zanini group in 1990, who felt an updated version of the middleweight twins could find a market. A chassis with a beam frame was developed by Nico Bakker and the 8-valve twins fitted with fuel injection and stretched to 668cc. But perhaps half a dozen of the resulting 650 Sports were built before the project collapsed. And then the Breganze factory was gone – today, a near-abandoned ruin, although the agricultural equipment arm of Laverda lives on nearby.

Industrialist and motorcycle enthusiast Francesco Tognon bought the ashes of Laverda, but abandoned Bregan-

A fine selection, which includes the later, most sporting, SFC triple (orange, furthest from camera). Note white triple with Saxon frame.

ze for a new factory a few miles to the west. Built in the town of Zanè, these models are usually referred to by that name. But by the time the 650 Sport reached full production in 1994, the benchmarks had moved dramatically – the Laverda may have handled well but the world had now seen the Ducati 916 and Honda Fireblade. And the Zanè models never shook off a reputation for unreliability. In 1996, a revised engine featuring water-cooling and 750cc was offered, but it could not compete as exotica against the Ducati 748, nor against the cheaper Japanese options on performance. Despite this, Laverda commissioned the design of a new triple that was shown to the public but would never become a Laverda; instead the prototype passed to the reborn Benelli factory as the Tornado.

But perhaps the greatest Laverda of all was the V6, an incredible motorcycle that was twice promised to buyers, never to materialize. The first occasion was in 1975, when a select handful of Laverda owners were told there was a new motorcycle being designed in Breganze that would be as astounding as it was audacious. A world-beater and a Jota-eater, with a price to match. Beyond that they were sworn to secrecy. It was 1977 before *Motorcycle News* broke the story that the new Laverda was a sporting V6 but they would not be road legal, and would cost four times the price of a Jota. Massimo Laverda had commissioned famed Maserati engine designer Giulio Alfieri who proposed a 996cc V6 to Laverda, suggesting a modular approach that would allow for a future V4 and V-twin. The idea was to build a racing motorcycle first, developing it on track, while generating publicity for a future road-going sports tourer.

Perhaps the most impressive part of the design was the pent roof combustion chamber with an ultra-shallow 24-degree included valve angle. To put that in perspective, most motorcycles were running between 80 and 60 degrees at the time, Ducati only putting a 25-degree degree head – the Testastretta – into production in 2001. After minor tuning, the first dynamometer runs produced 140bhp at 11,800rpm – 25bhp more than Honda's factory RCB endurance racers. Laverda had an excellent pedigree in endurance events, so plans were made to unveil the prototype V6 dressed for 24h racing at the 1977 Milan show. Unsurprisingly, the V6 was the star of the show with a chassis as radical as the motor, something that looked like a cross between an Egli but with twin shock-absorbers under the gearbox, compressed by a rocker arm on a swinging arm that also enclosed the shaft drive. This kept the wheelbase down to 59in, still long by the standards of the day.

Most of the motorcycle industry assumed that the V6 would remain a show bike. So when the V6 turned up at Paul Ricard for the 1978 Bol d'Or, surprise turned to shock when the Laverda proved to be the fastest bike on track by some margin. At 176mph (283km/h) the V6 was 20mph (32km/h) faster than the works Hondas, although at 520lb (236kg) it was really far too heavy for racing. After eight hours the universal joint on the shaft

One of only two Laverda V6s in existence. One is owned by Piero Laverda, this was built from a display model and parts by Cor Dees.

A late 750cc front, a 1200cc Mirage centre and an early 750cc behind that.

drive failed, although it was repaired and brought back out for the televised final hour.

But development was always going to be hard for a firm of Laverda's size and the hope of a V6 racer was killed when endurance racing became a world championship in 1980, meaning that four cylinders would be the maximum allowed. Yet in 1990, hopes of a production V6 were raised again. As well as promising to put updated middleweight twins into production, Zanini announced there would be a limited run of twenty-five road-legal V6s, closely modelled on the Bol d'Or racer. When only nineteen people placed deposits, Laverda put the price up, and when every subsequent buyer bailed out, Laverda asked for more from

those left standing. In the meantime, Laverda were struggling with quality control on the bikes they were actually building. Eventually, Laverda simply sold out to Aprilia.

Given that the V6 Zanini showed was really a collection of spares, and that Cor Dees, who owned the Dutch Laverda museum, struggled to get his V6 built, it seems unlikely the V6 road bikes could have been delivered at any price. But to show what a place they hold in Laverda fans' imaginations, when Cor sold his museum, he kept just one motorcycle – the V6.

So apart from a few 'Laverda SFCs' – glorified Aprilia Milles, built in a fit of hubris before all fell under Piaggio control – that will probably be the end of the marque. In

The V6 had an unusual swing arm design to minimize wheelbase.

theory, Piaggio could announce a new Laverda range at any time, but in truth, do not need competition for Aprilia's sports bikes, especially as that is a market in decline. But Laverda will live on in the hearts of anyone who appreciates fast motorcycles with a sporting edge.

LAZZATI (1898–04)

Perhaps the first entirely Italian motorcycle. The patent claims a motor with just 0.2bhp, but a speed of 25mph (40km/h). Built in Milan.

LECCE (1929–32)

One of the very few factories in the south of Italy based in Lecce, Puglia. Founder Otello Albanese had wanted to use his own 3-cylinder engine but, lacking the necessary resources, used a 175cc Swiss Moser modified with a single inlet but twin exhaust valves.

LEGNANO – *SEE* WOLSIT

LEPROTTO (1951–57)

Overhead-valve, single-cylinder motorcycles of 125cc, 160cc and 200cc, built in Turin.

LINTO (1967–70)

Lino Tonti's own motorcycles. In 1937, he joined Benelli, working with Giuseppe Benelli on the 250cc four, using his training as a radio and electrical engineer to develop systems such as the ignition. But post-war, Lino mastered a full range of engineering skills alongside friends who were converting decommissioned military Triumph 350 singles into road bikes. Inevitably, he took to tuning racing motorcycles that enjoyed success in the hands of privateers. Lino soon established a company to build motorcycles, Orim, co-founded with his uncle, but a short-lived venture. Instead he is remembered mostly for his work with Aermacchi, Bianchi, Moto Guzzi and Paton.

Linto was a contracting and tuning factory, as much as a manufacturer. Aermacchi's relationship with Linto was similar to that of Ducati and NCR in the 1970s. Aermacchi's works enduro riders often sported Linto sweaters in recognition of Lino Tonti's contribution to the development and preparation of their motorcycles.

But Lino is best known for his Linto 500 – often called a 'double Aermacchi 250', because so many parts from the Varese firm's 250 Ala d'Oro production racer were used. Lino started the project in 1966, initially intending no connection with Aermacchi. He wanted to build a twin-cylinder, 500cc GP racer with double overhead-camshafts and four radial valves per cylinder, but soon realized the project would not be economically viable. His idea rested on building something not much more expensive than the British singles, but with a chance of keeping the MV Agustas in sight.

Lino Tonti's 500cc twin-cylinder Linto, essentially a pair of Aermacchi 250s.

So, Lino decided to build an engine using existing parts from the Aermacchi Harley-Davidson 250 Ala d'Oro. But, in 1967, he joined Moto Guzzi, which slowed his own project's development to a crawl. Yet he persevered, thanks to people such as his assistant Alcide Biotti and former racer Umberto Premoli, who helped with funding.

1969 was the most successful year for the Linto. Tonti offered Jack Findlay a Linto 500 in a sponsorship deal. Along with Nello Pagani and Swiss rider Guyla Marsovszky, Findlay made up the trio of riders most associated with the Linto 500. In just the second race of the season, the German Grand Prix at the ultra-fast Hockenheim circuit, Findlay surprised the competition by finishing third, only beaten by Agostini's MV and German Hockenheim specialist Karl Heinz Hoppe on a Metisse. Until then any success the Linto enjoyed had been attributed to Pagani's expertise, but Findlay showed there was more to the motorcycle than that. Marsovszky was to underline the motorcycle's potential when he finished the 1969 season as runner-up in the world championship. Alberto Pagani also won the Italian Grand Prix that year on Tonti's twin. With 66bhp at 10,000rpm, the Linto delivered more power than the 500cc singles, even if it was not enough to match the 83bhp of the MV Agusta that Agostini should have been riding. Count Agusta was upset that Imola had been chosen as the circuit for the Italian Grand Prix, rather than

the Monza track. Count Agusta owned a house literally a stone's throw from that circuit's tarmac, which was also where MV tested. To make the FIM rethink their ruling, the Count withdrew his entry, gifting the Linto a win.

But the Linto's real failing was unreliability, in an age when an engine failure could be fatal. Findlay became concerned enough to give up the free use of the Linto, opting mid-season to ride his G50 Matchless-powered Seeley instead. Linto never again achieved the heights they had reached in 1969. In 1970, the Italian Grand Prix returned to Monza to be won by Agostini on an MV Agusta. The more things change, the more they stay the same.

LINX (1929–41)

Milan-based, using a wide variety of British motors, including 175cc Python Rudge, 350cc Blackburne and 500cc JAP.

LIVIA (1932–35)

Based in Padua west of Venice, the motorcycles of Guido Lotto and Bruno Ghisellini powered by 98cc and 125cc Sachs engines.

MAFFEIS (1903–35)

Brothers Miro, Carletto and Bernardo Maffeis may have built a motorcycle as early as 1895 in their Porta Volta workshops in northern Milan. All three were successful racers and, in 1903, Carletto won the Susa-Mont Cenis on a Sarolea, although his career would end tragically 1921 at the Circuit de Brescia.

Miro, the youngest brother, began racing in 1919, first with Motosacoche but then with many others, including Indian, Harley-Davidson and Gilera. He also raced the first Maffeis designed by Bernard. Miro used his Maffeis to win the 250cc class of the Italian Championship at the Circuito del Lario in 1923, 1924 and 1925. Maffeis also won the 250 class at the German Grand Prix dell'Avus. He would also race for, and be a test rider for, Bianchi

Manufacture of the production Maffeis began in 1903, using engines by Sarolea, Minerva and Barscott. By 1921, they were offering an in-house designed and built 350cc overhead-valve, V-twin with a three-speed gearbox. From 1923, Blackburne engines were an option, and ten years later all were badged as Miro Maffeis, with the sole surviving brother, Miro, joining forces with Aurelio and Enrico Tornielli.

MAGLIANO (1948–49)

Mario and Luigi Magliano used their motorcycle to set eight world records in the 75cc and 100cc classes. They were double overhead-cam engines in a partially faired motorcycle built for the task.

MAGNI (1928–30)

A 350cc parallel twin with shaft-driven, overhead-cam built in Milan by Luigi Magni. He never achieved mass production. Later, he also built a single-cylinder overhead-valve 500cc.

MAGNI (1977–)

Arturo Magni was central to MV's racing success from the moment he and engine-designer, Piero Remor, left Gilera for MV. Both were poached by Count Domenico Agusta in 1950 for his struggling race team. Rising to assume total responsibility for the company's racing efforts, Arturo turned MV into a dominant force. When

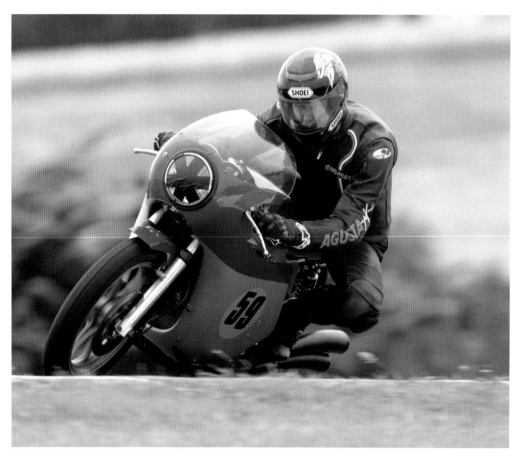

This MV Agusta America features almost everything Arturo Magni offered: chain rather than shaft drive and a big bore kit.
RUSS MURRAY

An early Sfida. Note the 'Parallelogrammo' rear suspension designed to minimize the effect of shaft drive on handling.

For some, the ultimate Moto Guzzi and/or Magni: the Australia.

the MV factory retired from racing in 1977, he and his sons began to modify road-going MVs with new frames, chain drive and bodywork. These are perhaps the ultimate road-going classic MVs. Initially, Magni produced components that effectively allowed owners to turn their road bikes into a 1960s' MV grand prix racer with either an 832cc or 868cc engine. There were frames, chain-drive conversion, bodywork, brakes, forks, magnesium wheels, suspension and engine upgrades. Some may argue that there is also the Monza (also known as the Boxer, 850SS or Super Daytona, depending on which country

the bike was to be sold in) but it would be fairer to say this is basically a modified America with only a few bikes leaving the Magni factory near Varese and the remainder being either dealer or owner modified.

However, as there was a limited number of MV fours, Magni turned its attention to first modifying Hondas, then BMWs, Moto Guzzis and Suzukis. There was even a minimoto and a Triumph/BSA triple-powered special.

Honda power was from the 16-valve, twin-cam four, ultimately superseded by a Suzuki a 1200 Bandit motor around the year 2000. There were fewer than 150 of the BMW R100-powered version that became available around 1980.

In 1985, Magni started a relationship with Moto Guzzi, initially developing a Le Mans with *Parallelogrammo* rear suspension to eliminate the shaft-drive reactions. For 1987, there were complete bikes, the Classico and Arturo 1000s and, in 1989, the *Sfida* (Challenge). For 1990, this had Daytona 4-valve heads and, such was its success for Owen Coles, it was entered by Australian Moto Guzzi importer Ted Stolarski in races in Australia, New Zealand and the USA. Consequently, Magni named the subsequent production model demanded by Stolarski the Australia. Production began in 1993 of a monoshock version with 2-valve heads and carburettors of which seventy-five were built. For 1998, a 4-valve, 102bhp model with Weber Marelli fuel-injection and revised chassis was dubbed the Australia 98. Only fifty were made.

Arturo Magni passed away in 2005, but Magni carry on today with new models based on the current MV Agusta's 3-cylinder engines.

MAININI (1966–70)

Mainini were, from 1947, motorcycle dealers in Busto Arsizio, between Milan and Varese. In 1966, they built a racing 125cc powered by a downsized Aermacchi 175. They followed this up with an Aermacchi racing two-stroke 125cc converted from piston port to disc valve, allowing a 32mm carburettor. It was housed in a chassis designed by Othmar Drixl that weighed 24lb (11kg) less than the Aermacchi version.

MAJOR (1947–49)

Turin-built, single-cylinder, overhead-valve 350cc designed by Salvatore Majorca, who previously worked at Fiat. But it is the appearance of the motorcycle that is most interesting: a full fairing designed to minimize fatigue and maximize fuel consumption. The styling and fittings would look sensational if it were launched today.

MALAGUTI (1923–)

Founded by Antonio Malaguti, making bicycles, and abandoned during the Second World War. Like Bologna neighbours, Ducati (who would help them enter the US market), during the 1950s Malaguti looked at producing anything that might make a profit, including washing

machines and bicycles with the Garelli Mosquito motor. Later models were powered by Franco Morini two-strokes. During the Vietnam War, Vietnam was Malaguti's biggest market and their first 50cc scooter was called the Saigon. Apart from a brief flirtation with a 125cc two-stroke, Malaguti focused on the 50cc market. During the oil crisis, the US became a big market for fuel-sipping mopeds, but for British riders, it will be the Olymique sports moped that is most remembered. With clip-ons, a huge fuel tank and bum stop seat, it was one of the ultimate 'sixteens' electronically tested by *Bike* magazine at over 52mph (82km/h).

During the 1990s, Malaguti were often in the top three Italian scooter manufactures, now using Yamaha engines of up to 150cc, but post the 11 September 2001 attacks their US sales collapsed.

Despite – or because of – this, Malaguti entered MotoGP with a brand new 125cc from 2003 to 2006, but without notable success. Hit, like all other Italian firms, by the 2004 helmet laws, Malaguti finally folded as a manufacturer but live on as a spares' business.

MALANCA (1956–86)

Mario Malanca began producing wheel hubs in his workshop in Bologna, debuting the first Malanca in 1956, using a Franco Morini 50cc motor. From 1960, Malanca were making their own 50cc two-strokes and, ultimately, a 125cc twin from 1974, which became liquid-cooled in 1982.

But it is Malanca's racing history that deserves most attention. Walter Villa and Otello Buscherini started racing for Malanca in 1968 and over a five-year period the Malanca stable took six Italian championships in the 50cc and 60cc classes.

From 1972, Malanca competed in the 50 and 125 World Championships with two wins for Buscherini in 1973, and an overall fourth place in 1974, the final year Malanca contested the 50cc class. The final year for racing the 125 was 1976.

MARCHAND (1889–1909)

Originally, Paolo and Leone Marchand's bicycle factory in Milan, later moving to Piacenza and joining forces with Attilio Orio to build motorcycles. They soon became one of the best-known marques in Italy thanks to the racing exploits of Giuseppe Tamagni. All were single-cylinder, four-strokes with either automatic or two-speed gearboxes. The original model was rated at 1.75bhp and subsequent models (sold as the Magnet) at 2.5 and 3.5bhp.

MARIANI (1930–34)

A vertical single built by Enrico Mariani in Monzain 1930. It had three side-valves, perhaps a unique specification. The premise was that having been started on petrol, it could then run on naphthalene. Drive was via a three-speed Burman gearbox.

MAS (1928–56)

MAS (Motocicli Alberico Seiling) was founded in Milan. Early models had 148cc, 173cc and 244cc singles with overhead- and side-valve options and external flywheels. Pre-war, the focus switched to economic 248cc, 348cc and 568cc side-valve models, alongside a sole luxury touring model with an overhead-valve 498cc single. Most late 1930s' models offered rear suspension and all models had inclined cylinders.

During the war, MAS supplied militarized versions of the 498cc single and a 173cc two-stroke. Post-war, the Stella Alpina, a 125cc, had odd vertical finning intended to keep it cool in traffic. It was not a success, so MAS turned to more conventional overhead-valve and overhead-cam 175s. An overhead-cam 500 twin with racing ambitions never got beyond the prototype stage and MAS was reduced to making 125cc two-strokes and a Sachs powered 49cc mini-scooter.

MASERATI (1947–61)

This part of the Maserati family empire started as a manufacturer of motoring components. By purchasing Italmoto's Bologna factory in 1953, then making an overhead-valve 160cc single, Maserati instantly became a motorcycle manufacturer. Initially, Maseratis were almost identical to the Italmoto but were quickly developed to include a Formula 3 version for racing and ultimately a 250cc single. There were also microvans and 50cc two-strokes but, ultimately, Maserati could not compete with the established manufacturers.

Maserati 250, an attempt by the family to diversify from cars.

MASONI (1991)

Tullio Masoni's beam-framed Sound of Singles racer with his own 600cc horizontal single.

MASSARINI (1922–24)

Based in Piacenza, south of Milan, they built four-strokes of 125cc and 175cc.

MAV (1975–80)

MAV (Motori Ausiliari Velocipedi) produced competition off-road motorcycles for the 50cc, 125cc and 250cc classes. Engines were made by Minarelli, Sachs and Hiro, respectively, with Villa 125cc and 250cc motors from 1979. The factory may have been a continuation of a moped manufacturer of the same name established in 1951.

MAXIMA – *SEE* FINZI

MAZZILLI (1970–76)

Giorgio Mazzilli's Sachs-engined RSC 125, built in Milan. The engine was tuned to give 18bhp, so as to be competitive in off-road sport.

MAZZUCHELLI (1925–)

Based in Milan and built motorcycles with German 198cc Alba engines until 1928. They continue today as racing crank manufacturers.

MBA – *SEE* MORBIDELLI

MDS (1954–62)

Milan factory founded by brothers Giacomo, Mario and Tonino Scoccimarro, who, in 1955, presented overhead-valve singles of between 65cc and 80cc to power mopeds and scooters.

ME (1953–55)

A range of 175cc motorcycles built in Bologna, variously specified with overhead-valves, overhead-camshafts and a twin-cam super sport.

MECCANICA NVB (1956–58)

Milan factory offering motorcycles, mopeds and vans with two-stroke engines of 50cc and 150cc, and a 125cc four-stroke engine.

MEDUSA (1957–58)

175cc twin-cam parallel twin built in Milan by racer Vasco Loro from a design by Luciano Pasini. Intended for competition, it seems it was never entered into a race.

MELDI (1927–37)

Founded by Giuseppe Meldi in Turin, building principally racing machines with 248cc, 348cc and 498cc, overhead-valve JAP or Python engines. Meldi would later collaborate with Antonio Baudo at BM.

MELLO (1931–48)

Albino and Giuseppe 'Pinot' Mello were based in Valle Mosse, north of Turin. Initially using 250cc JAP engines, they quickly switched to Rudge and Mercury engines of 350cc and 500cc. During the war, Mello was a bicycle manufacturer and, in the immediate post-war period, their motorcycles had Triumph engines and transmissions. A twin exhaust 175cc was announced but probably never built.

MEMINI (1946–48)

Turin factory offering a 123cc two-stroke.

MENICUCCI – *SEE* PERUGINA

MENON (1875–32)

Originally, blacksmith and entrepreneur Carlo Menon's bicycle factory in Roncade, north of Venice. Although he did build an early small car, the first motorized bicycles were not produced until after the First World War. By the 1930s, 175s with JAP side-valve engines were available. A forward-sloping, single-cylinder 198cc four-stroke was also available, possibly built in-house as was a 350cc single. The family business, Menon Titanium, lives on as an engine valve manufacturer.

MERLI (1929–31)

Based in Parma, building motorcycles with 173cc two-stroke Train engines.

MERLONGHI (1923–28)

Founded in Tolentino, south of San Marino, to build an auxiliary motor, it was 1925 before the 98cc and 132cc two-stroke motorcycles were offered. Versions of these were used to set standing start kilometre records.

METEORA (1953–80)

Angelo Zanasi built the first Meteora using an overhead camshaft 175cc OMS engine in Monteveglio, Bologna. From 1955, Meteora fitted FB, NSU and Franco Morini engines from 50cc to 125cc.

In 1975, they started building Motobécanes for the French, Italian, German and US markets, building around 15,000 over the following five years. In 1980, Meteora ceased to offer mopeds under their own name, instead building models for Malaguti, Malanca and Moto Villa. Ultimately, they would assemble Hondas from parts imported from Japan. Now moved to Zola Predosa, near Bologna what remains of Meteora assembles for LEM and Beta.

MFB (1957–64)

Based in Bologna, they offered 50cc to 125cc two-strokes and an overhead-cam 175cc. All powered by Minarelli.

MG (1921–50)

Founded in Modena by Vittorio Guerzoni, initially using Train engines. In 1932, it was taken over by Guarinoni-Marinoni, who began building 250cc and 500cc with overhead camshafts. In 1933, almost identical models were sold under the Taurus banner from 1933 to 1947. After the war, the Taurus-built mopeds and motorcycles, including an overhead-cam 175cc and 250cc, and a two-stroke 160cc. MG was taken over by the Bergamini brothers who built 250cc and 500cc motorcycles branded as Centaurus.

MGF (1921–25)

Motocicli Garanzini Francesco (MGF) was based in Milan. Before establishing MGF, Francesco and his brother Orsete probably built motorcycles together under the brand name Verus. Then they built as Oreste & Garanzini, Garanzini-JAP, while Francesco used the MGF brand name. He built 248cc, 348cc and 498cc Blackburne side- and overhead-valve engines and a three-speed transmission. There is also mention of using Bekamo engines, as well as building motors to sell to others. Each model was produced in a Touring and Sport version.

MG/MGF (1921)

Motocicli Garanzini Francesco, based in Milan. Models included 250cc, 350cc and 500cc singles with Blackburne engines and three-speed gearboxes.

MIGNON (1922–32)

Mignon (also Moto Mignon Modena and often badged MMM) was the first motorcycle manufacturer in Modena. Founded by Vittorio Guerzoni, initially they produced a 123cc clip-on engine for bicycles, but from 1925 he was offering an overhead-valve 175cc single and 246cc parallel twin based upon Guerzoni's 125.

Vittorio Guerzoni so impressed Enzo Ferrari (who had a motorcycle race team pre-war) that in 1932 he smuggled Piero Taruffi's championship-winning Norton into his workshop and commissioned a motorcycle that could beat it. The first attempt was a twin-cam single with separate chains to each camshaft, replaced by a more Norton-line, bevel-drive, single-cam. Yet the result was no match for the Norton or the Rudges that Ferrari already had, so the project was abandoned. Guerzoni gave up Mignon to join Taurus/MG.

MILLER BALSAMO (1921–59)

Founded in 1921 by Ernesto and Edgardo Mario Balsamo in Milan, initially as importers of Excelsior and Ariel motorcycles. Their own motorcycles started with a 125cc and a 175cc powered by Moser or Python motors. An unsuccessful cyclemotor followed and then Python-engined 250, 350 and 500s. A lightweight 98cc Sachs was also offered and, eventually, an in-house-built 250cc. This was revised post-war alongside a new 125cc.

MINARELLI (1957–)

Vittorio Minarelli, having left FBM, started on his own account building up to seventy engines a day. The most famous, to motorcyclists, are the 50cc two-strokes but there were other applications. In 1967, the name changed again to Motori Minarelli, as it moved to new premises next to Bologna airport. By the 1970s, some annual production was up to 200,000 engines for two-wheelers and 50,000 for agricultural purposes. This allowed Minarelli to go chasing titles and records, most notably four 125 World Championships between 1978 and 1981 with Ángel Nieto.

By the 1990s, Minerelli were working with Yamaha, also building 50cc and 125cc two-strokes for Aprilia, Malaguti, Beta and Rieju, amongst others. Since 2002, they have been wholly owned by Yamaha but continue to build a range of engines, now mainly four-stroke singles in Bologna under the Yamaha Minarelli banner.

MINERVA (1929)

Side- and overhead-valve 175s built in Turin. No connection with the Belgian marque of the same name.

MINETTI (1924–27)

The Minetti brothers built a 124cc two-stroke in Turin.

MINIMOTOR (1945–56)

Turin manufacturer of mopeds, mentioned here because the Minimotor engine, designed by Vincenzo Piatti, was particularly successful in Britain.

MI-VAL (1943–95)

Metalmeccanica Italiana Valtrompia (Mi-Val based in

Minerelli for the most part made engines for others but occasionally offered complete motorcycles, usually racers.

Gardone Val Trompia, north of Brescia) started out as a manufacturer of machine tools, including for Beretta. The first motorcycle was produced in 1950 (125 T) and was a nearly perfect copy of DKW 125. The two-stroke 125s and 175s that followed were essentially a revision of this, with overhead-cam 175s and 200s coming later. There were three-wheelers and 50s, including supplying Norman for its Nippy III moped. Motorcycle manufacture ceased in 1966, and Mi-Val folded in 1995.

MM (1922–57)

Founded by Mario Mazzetti and Alfonso Morini in Bologna and debuting in 1924 with a 125cc single-cylinder, two-stroke that would enjoy competition success, notably in the 1925 Milano-Taranto where they were placed 10th and 13th in a field of mostly 350s and 500s. In 1929, a 175cc four-stroke was introduced, replaced by a 250cc in 1933. Further racing success followed, notably a class win in the 1940 Milano-Taranto. But financial problems and poor decisions stalked the business and, post-war, an attempt to revive the original 125cc as an economy motorcycle was not enough to save MM.

MOLARONI (1921–27)

Originally offering a 300cc two-stroke, vertical, single with a Sturmey Archer gearbox, they soon doubled up to create a 600cc flat-twin. There were 300cc and 350cc four-stroke singles built in the Pesaro factory from 1925.

MOLTENI – *SEE* FM

MONACO – *SEE* BAUDO

MONTÙ (1903–10)

Based south-west of Milan in Alessandria, using Sachs engines from 50cc to 175cc.

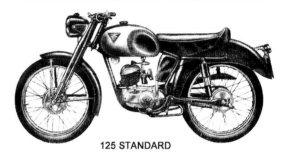

125 STANDARD

250 TURISMO

Note the effort to keep 125cc prices comparatively low, and how expensive were super sport models intended for racing, even without a tachometer (*senza contagiri*).

MONVISO (1951–56)

Motorcycles built in Savigliano west of Alessandria, again using Sachs engines of between 100cc and 175cc.

MORBIDELLI (1967–82)

Quiet, quick to smile and delightful company, Giancarlo Morbidelli used a hard earned fortune not for the predictable signallers of wealth, but to take on the Japanese factories in the crucible of world championship racing.

Pesaro, on Italy's Adriatic coast, was famously home to the Benelli factory, now converted into a modest museum. A little further out of the city, however, is the near mythical Morbidelli museum. Giancarlo Morbidelli made some fine woodworking machinery, but his real

love was always motorcycles, especially racing Benellis: 350cc motorcycles are on display alongside much more – including the Formula 1 car Morbidelli's son raced. Supporting him in this was one reason the Morbidelli race team was disbanded.

Astounded by everything from 1920s' Moto Guzzis, a Ducati 125 4-cylinder prototype, through to 1980s' race bikes, you might miss the arches at the far end of the main hall. Stepping through them is to step into another world: no longer are you among bikes chosen and restored out of respect for what others have achieved; this hall features Snr Morbidelli's race bikes. Not ones he just owns, but the ones he conceived, built and won world titles with – from 50cc through to the gorgeous 500cc four, they are surely the jewels in the crown.

The museum building was once home to Giancarlo Morbidelli's business empire, which explains how he funded race teams. Born in Pesaro in 1934, eldest son of a peasant family, Morbidelli attended technical college before working in a machinery factory. Eventually, with few resources but with great intelligence and determination, Morbidelli opened a small factory in Pesaro producing specialized woodworking machinery. It was soon a very successful business, employing over 300 people, and Morbidelli was now able to choose a different path. Given that Morbidelli decided to go racing rather than build road bikes, it is probably also safe to assume he had

a sneaking admiration of Count Agusta and his grand prix dominating MV Agusta fire engines.

The first bike carrying Morbidelli's own name into competition was a 1967 50cc racer using a frame design of his own, proprietary cycle parts and a Benelli engine. Racing became Morbidelli's temple of the mind, allowing him and his engineers' free reign alongside ideas of his own, as they sought to build bikes to bring trophies and even world titles home. Along the way there would be disappointment and tragedy: the loss of Gilberto Parlotti, who perished racing in a fog-bound TT while leading the 125 World Championship, must have cut deep into the thoughtful and gentle Giancarlo Morbidelli. But hard work and application bring their own rewards and, in 1975, the team carried off their first 125 World Championship with Paolo Pileri.

It was at this point that Morbidelli Benelli Armi (MBA) was formed to sell what were effectively replica 125 and 250 Morbidelli twins to privateers. Benelli Armi was the gun-making division that had not been part of the family's sale of Benelli to De Tomaso. Early MBAs were problematic, but the 125s especially became fast and reliable, taking the 1978 and 1980 world championships. After this, MBA ended direct entries into grand prix, the race department moving to Sanvenero (see Sanvenero). MBA became the privateer's perfect partner and around 700 were eventually sold. The end came when the FIM decid-

The first ever Morbidelli: a 50cc racer.

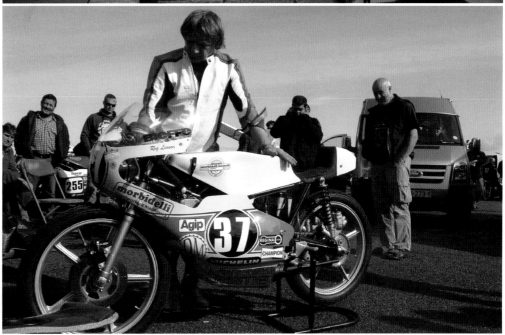

An MBA, effectively a privateers' Morbidelli, being warmed up at Jurby on the Isle of Man.

ed to limit 125s to a single cylinder for the 1987 European Championship and for the 1988 World Championship. That killed MBA, not the quality of their motorcycles, although they had outlived their Morbidelli parent.

Back to 1977, the year that Morbidelli really took off, winning not only the 125 title with Pier Paolo Bianchi, but also the 250 trophy with Mario Lega. No doubt Count Agusta would have approved, as his MV team abandoned grand prix racing, if Morbidelli would fill the shoes he had vacated in the blue riband 500 class.

By the end of 1977, Giancarlo Morbidelli had the money and engineering staff to build race winners, with three constructors and four rider's world championships to his name. But far from resting on his laurels and sticking to the smaller classes, Giancarlo moved his team up a gear.

The result was the rare and beautiful Morbidelli 500cc two-stroke grand prix racers that carried a now famous name into battle from 1979 to 1982.

It would be doing the Morbidelli team an injustice to suggest they copied other designs for their 500cc, although they did use a modified TZ750 rolling chassis for early engine tests. Morbidelli continued using the lessons learnt on the smaller capacity bikes – the first 500cc engine in many ways a doubling up of their 250cc. It was, as was now expected of Morbidelli, an exercise in original thinking with clever aerodynamics and beautiful engineering.

Certainly the bike was a square four of 54 × 54mm dimensions with rotary valves, like the Suzuki RG500, but using two rather than the Suzuki's four crankshafts.

The far hall of the Morbidelli Museum has the eponymous racers. Notice how Morbidelli were years ahead of anyone else in using aerodynamics, from solid wheels to large tailpieces, intended to tidy up airflow leaving the bike.

With the heads canted forward by 35 degrees and an underslung gearbox, this was a well thought-out and compact power unit. The magnesium alloy parts, notably engine cases, were supplied by Campagnolo on the first version raced in 1979. The frame was a conventional twin-loop, tubular steel design with alloy swinging arm carrying 18in wheels, also from Campagnolo, with Brembo brakes. One thing Morbidelli was very interested in was aerodynamic efficiency, so the bike sported a boxy looking rear end, very similar to their 125 and 250s. Much of this was developed in collaboration with California's Santa Anna University, allowing students to better understand the dynamics of airflow. Philippe de Lespinay was hired in 1977 to provide new ideas based on previous work he had begun in 1968, sketching motorcycle concepts derived from the Ray Amm 1953 Norton kneeler. Some of these ideas were truly radical, including a feet-forward 500cc with the rider sitting in front of the engine to minimize frontal area. Approaching the FIM to query the legality of the layout, they were told in no uncertain terms it would never be allowed. But such thinking shows how Morbidelli sought to gain an advantage wherever he could.

Picking the rider for the new motorcycle seems to have been the easy part. Riding Morbidelli's 250cc in 1979 was Graziano Rossi (Valentino's father), promoted to riding the 500cc as well. Both he and Giancarlo being local to Pesaro cemented the deal for Morbidelli: a few miles away in the hills above Pesaro is the Rossi family's home village of Tavullia. Even so, with his trademark wild hair and beard, Graziano was hardly in the mould of then current world champion, Kenny Roberts.

The team made its 500cc debut at Hockenheim – round three – Rossi qualifying the bike twelfth in the days when there could be almost forty entrants. Rossi's qualifying time was 2.1sec shy of fastest man Barry Sheene on the works Suzuki. A good start but, disappointingly, finishing out of the points at race's end. Although Rossi was mentioned in *Motocourse* as 'impressively fast', he had no luck on the 250cc either.

Round four was closer to home at Imola, and a points-scoring ninth place merited another mention in *Motocourse*, with 'Rossi giving a striking account of himself and the new Morbidelli'. Disappointingly, his 250cc broke while leading, causing some to ask if Morbidelli were stretching themselves too thinly.

For the next meeting in Spain, *Motocourse* eulogized about 'the performance of Rossi's Morbidelli… lying just behind Ferrari [Virginio, on an RG500] when it finally failed after sixteen laps'. Ferrari finished fourth. Rossi had already finished third in the 250cc race, the 350cc contest usually splitting the 250s and 500s, giving him some recovery time. Then it was to Rijeka in Yugoslavia, a long-forgotten setting for a grand prix, although Rossi will remember it. He crashed at half-distance, struggling with the 500's weight. He made amends in the 250cc race by winning. Next stop was Assen, and another twelfth place for the 500cc and Rossi's second 250cc win on the trot.

But from here the season went downhill, with Rossi proving crash-prone and the Morbidellis occasionally un-

The monocoque 500cc, raced by Valentino Rossi's father, using the fuel tank as part of the frame.

reliable. By 1979, it was rare for a rider to be asked to race twice in a day, especially on such different bikes. The Morbidelli 500 was also heavy compared to the Japanese competitors, never mind the 250. Still, Rossi finished third in the 250 championship, but thirty-third (of forty) in the 500 class must have been crushing.

Far from being crushed by the effort of running a 250cc and a 500cc, Morbidelli had been accumulating radical ideas. Over the winter there was a revolution in Morbidelli's race shop. The old 500's heavy motor was replaced with a new, over square 55 × 52mm four. The cylinders were now set in a shallow 45-degree Vee, producing a very respectable 130bhp, and weighing a lot less.

But it was the frame that really showed the design team's originality, debuting an alloy monocoque frame for which this evolution of the Morbidelli 500 is most famous. The monocoque included a fuel cell and the engine hung from rear mounts. Giancarlo Morbidelli explained that when he first brought the monocoque 500 into the pits, a very excited Kawasaki technician appeared and started taking photographs, the implication being the monocoque KR500 was inspired by Morbidelli. But subsequent checking has the Kawasaki, like the Morbidelli, debuting in the world championship's season opener at Misano Adriatico on 11 May 1980.

The early Morbidelli monocoques had a convention twin rear shock-absorber layout but these were soon replaced by a cantilever system, with a six-bar linkage and two bell cranks, giving a genuinely progressive rising rate

suspension. Although observers at the time thought it an over-complex solution, no-one else had anything quite like it.

What Morbidelli no longer had was Graziano Rossi, who had left to ride for Nava Olio Fiat Suzuki under Roberto Gallina. By the end of the 1980 season, Rossi would prove his class with fifth overall in the 500 championship. Morbidelli replaced Rossi with journeyman Giovanni Pellettier, who had spent 1979 aboard an RG500 Suzuki with a best result of tenth place in the Italian Grand Prix.

Pelletier did bring Morbidelli sponsorship from Bieffe helmets but it could not have lessened the shock of how poorly the team would fare in 1980. There was a single finish, twenty-first in Finland, scant reward for a heavy financial investment in new machinery. And, despite Graziano Rossi returning to ride the monocoque the following year, not a single finish was recorded for the 500 in 1981. Rossi eventually took eleventh place in the British Grand Prix, but riding a Yamaha 500, seemingly having given up on the Morbidelli. Once again, arguably the prettiest, and certainly one of the most innovative, motorcycles in the championship had failed to produce results.

The 1982 season was the last year Morbidelli raced motorcycles under his own name, citing 'economic realities' for the team's closure at the end of the season. Three finishes were recorded for the 500, the best a fifteenth in Germany. From the outside this episode in Morbidelli's history must look a glorious failure, but a quote attributed to Giancarlo Morbidelli says it all:

I do not have engineers [any more], and even if I did have, I would continue as I am now, losing nights thinking about how to build the engine and then seeing it born with my technicians, putting on a dirty coat and working with my mechanics. For me this is the real satisfaction.

Giancarlo's next motorcycle project was his 1994 V8, intended to be a luxurious tourer. Highly innovative, with shaft drive from a 32-valve, liquid-cooled, 847cc, 90-degree V8, it was the bodywork that caught everybody's eye. The work of car stylists Pininfarina, it gave the motorcycle a heavy, droopy look that could not justify the price tag of $60,000 – about five times as much as the newly released Ducati 916. Added to this was that servicing and repair work would involve shipping the V8 back to the Morbidelli. So, sadly, there were no takers, despite it being an engineering *tour de force*. But Giancarlo still tinkers with his hope for a follow-up V12.

If the 500 and V8 Morbidellis were a failure, the man who created them never was. Proof that Giancarlo Morbidelli meant all he said about 'putting on a dirty coat and working with my mechanics' is that, after walking away from racing, he sold his woodworking machinery empire and started to restore a remarkable – no, simply astonishing – collection of motorcycles, with special emphasis

First hall in the Morbidelli museum. There are mainly Italian motorcycles, but not exclusively.

on his beloved Benellis. When you finally reach the end of the tour, there's yet another hall, but this time gloomy and grubby. Here there are the future projects, and tucked away somewhere is the V12 engine that moves on his dream of a V8 road bike. For a man who could have had the usual trappings of wealth – yachts, race horses, whatever – here is proof that he is an enthusiast, just like the rest of us.

Snr Morbidelli gathers a crowd around the V8.

Alternative view of the racing Morbidelli collection.

MOTO –

Some marques used this prefix inconsistently: if not listed here, look for the name without the prefix, e.g. Parilla rather than Moto Parilla.

MOTO BM (1952–88)

Bonvicini factory based in Rastignano Pianoro near Bologna. Lightweights powered by 125cc and 160cc ILO two-stroke engines. From 1953 to 1955, NSU four-stokes were added to the range from 75cc to 250cc, including a 250cc twin; and, from 1956, Minerelli-powered mopeds, also sold in Germany badged as Tonax.

MOTODELTA (1970–73)

Marque based near Florence. Their first machine was a 125cc motocrosser, but thereafter mainly mopeds.

MOTO EMILIA / ME (1953–55)

Short-lived Bolognese venture offering a 175cc with overhead valves and single or double overhead-cams.

MOTO GUZZI (1921–)

Established in Mandello del Lario by Carlo Guzzi and Giorgio Parodi, Moto Guzzi is a marque that, like Ducati, it is impossible to summarize here without major sins of omission. I have written a book on their history for Crowood, but even 60,000 odd words required many models to be omitted. Here, as with the Ducati entry, the story is better told with photographs.

The Moto Guzzi factory is probably the oldest to have continuously produced motorcycles in one place. Highlights are the horizontal singles, especially the 350 world championship machine, although it is inevitably overshadowed by the V8.

The biggest seller by far, however, was the Guzzino (Little Guzzi) and its variants. Antonio Micucci, overseen by Guzzi's resident genius Giulio Cesare Carcano, was instructed to design a motorcycle that would be a distinct

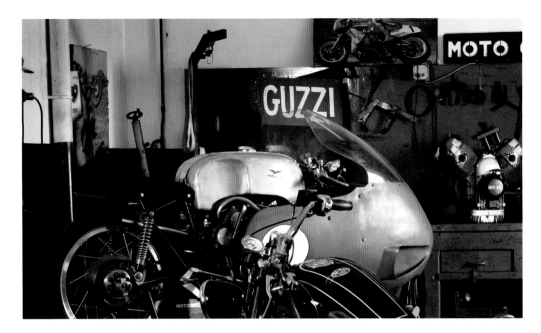

The V8 might be the most famous Moto Guzzi, but it was preceded by an odd longitudinal four with shaft drive. Like all Guzzis of the era, the obsession was with minimizing frontal area and using the wind tunnel to gain speed.
PIAGGIO / MOTO GUZZI

The Moto Guzzi factory – the oldest active motorcycle factory in the world.

– but affordable – step-up from the cyclemotors that were overrunning Italy. His answer was based around a 64cc rotary valve two-stroke that would give 2bhp, even on poor-quality fuel. Traditional Guzzi qualities included gear primary drive and a three-speed gearbox, and the all-alloy unit proved astoundingly reliable. Housed in a chassis that offered full suspension front and rear, with far more stability than a bicycle with a clip-on engine, the Guzzino was an instant hit when launched in 1946. Weighing in at a mere 45kg (100lb), the diminutive motorcycle was capable of 30mph (50km/h), which was just about enough for the market at which it was aimed. Production updates involved little more than renaming the bike Motoleggera 65 and astute re-engineering that allowed the price to be

reduced some 30 per cent by 1949, meaning the complete motorcycle cost less than twice what Ducati were asking for a 48cc motor alone. The baby Guzzi was utterly classless with 50,000 built in the first three years of production – a record in Italy. In 1951, the 65 became the Cardellino (goldfinch) with styling closer to a motorcycle, including a pillion seat. Over the years the capacity grew to first 73cc and then, finally in 1962, to 83cc before production ended in 1963. By then almost 215,000 variants had been built and the design licensed overseas, a phenomenal number of motorcycles by Italian manufacturing standards, and about half of Moto Guzzi's all-time production. Only Ducati's Monster has sold more units, but that has required regular re-invention over a much longer period.

The Guzzi Parodi of 1918, the first bike made in the factory. Financier Giorgio Parodi decided he did not want his name attached to the motorcycles in case the venture failed.

The Airone was in essence a 500cc with a smaller, 250cc, engine: cycle parts between the two models were very similar.

A new batch of 110cc Zigolo (Bunting) leave the factory. PIAGGIO/ MOTO GUZZI

119

Pre-war Moto Guzzi offered this vast inline four.

John Britten borrowed the Fossati Hotel's Guzzino. It seems doubtful he copied the blade forks for his own V-twin. HOTEL FOSSATI

The biggest Moto Guzzi myth is that Carcano's V-twin was built as a tractor engine: it was always intended for a motorcycle and, although some say it was intended for Abarth, that was the result of Carcano fitting the prototype engine to his company Fiat 500.

While it is true that Moto Guzzi built a V-twin for military vehicles, this was an entirely different engine designed by two-stroke specialist Micucci. When De Tomaso bought Moto Guzzi, he reportedly arrived at the factory waving a sword and shouting 'No more stupid

ABOVE: The Moto Guzzi Dondolino (colloquially rocking chair, a reference to the rear suspension) was an over-the-counter racer.

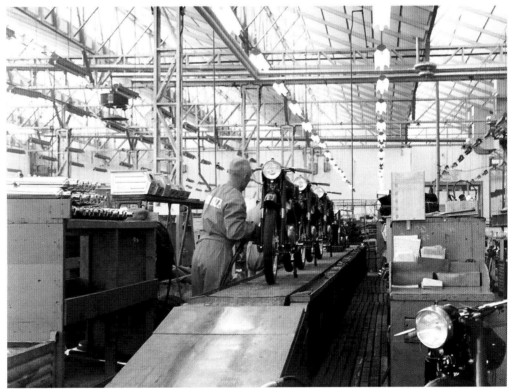

RIGHT: A production line. Moto Guzzi looked after their staff – there was even an on-site hospital.

PIAGGIO / MOTO GUZZI

twins'. Carcano talked him out of it and the result was the Le Mans. However, all the four-strokes of the De Tomaso Benelli/Moto Guzzi era were built in the Mandello del Lario factory, including Moto Guzzi-badged Seis. All the two-strokes, including those badged as Moto Guzzi, were built at the Benelli factory in Pesaro.

It is a shame Piaggio seem to view Moto Guzzi as a minor player, plans to make the factory a destination ho-

tel and retail experience failing to materialize. Given the popularity of Harley-Davidson in Italy, it would seem there is a market for the magnificent California range, and a place for a range between these and the small block 750s that are evolutions of the V50. But at least the factory and its wonderful museum is still there, a better fate than Piaggio allowed Laverda.

CLOCKWISE, FROM TOP LEFT:
Scooter and a successful ISDT version of the Stornello in the museum.

The famous wind tunnel. There is a publicity film showing it being used to fine-tune the MkII Le Mans.
PIAGGIO/APRILIA

The mighty V8. Note how comparatively narrow the fairing is.

The Bicilindrica 500 was more successful than the V8 would be. Stanley Woods used one to win the 1935 Senior TT, the first for a foreign motorcycle. He finished just 4sec ahead of Jimmie Guthrie's Norton after six laps – still the tightest margin in any TT.

Keith Campbell and the V8 in 1957, its final year of racing.

To compete with the other Italian factories, Moto Guzzi launched the 175cc overhead-cam Lodola (lark), the final design by Carlo Guzzi. It was soon replaced with a 235cc overhead-valve version.

The 500cc single also powered a series of lightweight trucks, perfect for narrow streets.

The V-twins were used in large touring motorcycles aimed at the US market.

It was Tonti who reframed the V-twin to create a much sportier motorcycle, which he used to set a number of speed records.

The French importer ran a V-twin with an automatic gearbox with some success in the Bol d'Or.

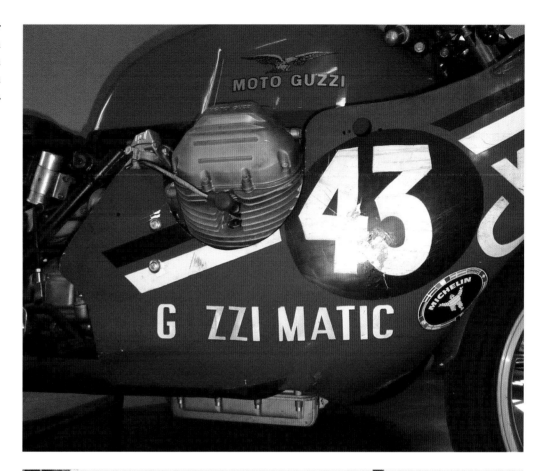

There was officially no MkI Le Mans: it was simply Le Mans. The early ones had the tail light within the rear mudguard fibreglass and a more humped seat. So the model pictured is, retrospectively, generally referred to as a second series MkI.

All the De Tomasos fours and sixes were made by Moto Guzzi, although most were badged as Benellis.

The 'small bock' V-twins started with the V35 and V50 made at the old Innocenti factory.

PIAGGIO / MOTO GUZZI

The small V-twins made very good dual-purpose models. Special versions were built for the Paris Dakar and the military.

RIGHT: The fashion for full enclosure briefly touched Moto Guzzi.

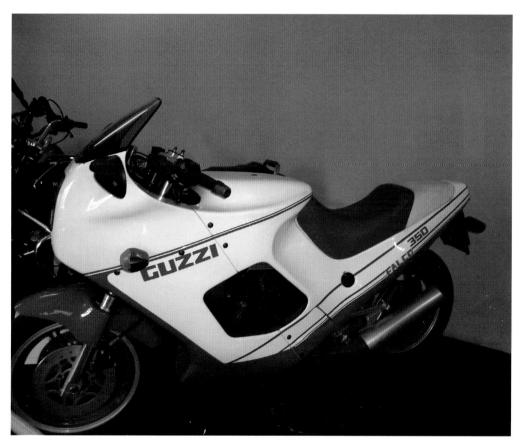

BELOW: The current range of all sub-1000cc Moto Guzzis can trace their roots to the V50, which was switched back to the Moto Guzzi factory. This is part of the 'Italian TT' course, the Circuito del Lario.

LEFT: **The current top of the range 750cc.** PIAGGIO/ MOTO GUZZI

BELOW: **The new range of 1380cc California's are charming, but huge and inevitably face a battle trying to steal sales from Harley-Davidson.** PIAGGIO/MOTO GUZZI

MOTO MORINI (1946–)

Founded in 1946 by Alfonso Morini, who had left MM in 1937 frustrated and ready to strike out on his own. The first Morinis were, therefore, unsurprisingly like MM models: a 125cc two-stroke and an overhead-valve 175cc that would evolve into the Settebello.

It is not often that a single model completely transforms a motorcycle manufacturer's luck, but Morini's Settebello is one: perhaps even one in a class of one. An evolution of Morini's first four-stroke, the overhead-valve, pushrod 175cc, sold so well that Morini had to build a new factory in Via Bergamo, Bologna, to cope with demand. Despite an outwardly prosaic specification, the Settebello was built with racing in mind, specifically the Milano-Taranto and the Motogiro. Engines came with a 25mm SSI Dell'Orto and a guarantee that the engine had been dynamometer-tested to be sure it was tuned to perfection. This was especially useful if you chose the controversial open-exhaust option.

The Settebello name is one of those peculiarities of Italian, meaning seven of diamonds (as in the playing card), even though *sette bello* is, literally, beautiful seven. Another peculiarity was that open-exhaust option, because Motogiro rules required silencers to be fitted. This led to MV Agusta and Parilla withdrawing from the 1954 Motogiro, protesting loudly that their quieter bikes were being penalized. That helped the Settebello take four of the top eight places, with Manganelli coming in second behind Provini's overhead-cam Mondial. The 175cc production class in the Milano-Taranto was not as fruitful: Tramelli's Settebello took third but, again, it was no match for the single overhead-cam Mondial. Morini's answer was the overhead-cam Rebello, probably the most advanced road bike of its time. Unhappily, the competition did not consider it a road bike: Morini dealers could offer nothing even vaguely resembling the Rebello, and Mondial immediately withdrew from the Motogiro in protest. MV Agusta did likewise when newspapers accused them of offering factory support to supposedly private entries.

The Rebello and rider, Emilio Mendogni, were therefore dominant in the 1955 Motogiro, winning seven of the nine legs. Mattei's Settebello took third, but the results were tainted by the protests and accusations that delayed Mendogni from being crowed victor for months. By then Mario Preta had scored a resounding class win for Morini in the Milano-Taranto, not only coming home almost 30min ahead of the second-in-class Bianchi 175, but taking second overall – only beaten by Francisci's Gilera 500 four. Third went to another Gilera four, underlining the Rebello's brilliance.

The Rebello bore little similarity to the Settebello, apart from the 175cc capacity. The chain-driven overhead-cam ran a tachometer, and there was a five-speed gearbox – almost unique at the time. The 27mm Dell'Orto carburettor helped Morini claim 22bhp at over 9,000rpm, and 105mph (169km/h) – excellent for a four-stroke 175cc single now, and incredible in 1955. The Rebello became so successful that it paved the way for the Motogiro's split classes (into production bikes

Although Morini are associated with four-strokes, like most Italian factories they offered cheaper two-stroke options. This 125cc, like the BSA Bantam, was based on the DKW.

Developed from the Motogiro winning 175cc, the Morini 250 grand prix racer almost beat Jim Redman and the Honda four to the world championship title. BONHAMS MOTORCYCLES

A 1956 Morini Settebello replica. THESUPERMAT

verses prototypes) that opened the door for the Ducati Mariana in 1956.

While the Rebello evolved into the twin-cam 250cc grand prix racer, the Settebello sired the Tresette (again named after playing cards, three and seven), a slower but more practical 175cc with a fibreglass tail piece. The Tresette was another strong seller from a factory that understood what its customers wanted better than anybody else. In 1950s Italy, customers wanted a 175cc that offered speed, style, reliability and with a home-servicing, friendly pushrod engine. Alfonso Morini was happy to oblige, and went on to reap the rewards.

Morini's first stab at a 250cc racer based on the Rebello was not as fast or as reliable as hoped, despite twin carburettors, twin cams and a five-speed gearbox. Alfonso Morini, therefore, started with a clean sheet of paper and long-time collaborator Dante Lambertini, joined by Nerio Biavati newly arrived from Mondial. The result was a motorcycle that took the first two places in its first race, the final round of the 1958 World Championship. Mendogni rode to victory on the 14 September in the Grand Prix of Nations at Monza, followed home by Giampiero Zubani.

The only common part between the old and new 250s was the twin-cam head. The vertical 72 × 61mm, 248cc single-cylinder engine gave an MV Agusta-matching 32bhp at 10,500rpm. Two sodium-filled valves set at 90 degrees in a twin-plug hemispheric chamber were fed by a 30mm Dell'Orto carburettor. A dry sump sat below a primary gear-drive, a dry clutch and a six-speed gearbox. Magnesium alloy crankcases and covers helped get the weight down to 113kg.

Alfonso Morini chose Tarquinio Provini to be his sole rider, which proved a wise decision when Provini won the 1961 and 1962 Italian 250 Championships, becoming convinced that the motorcycle could beat much tougher odds. Despite Alfonso Morini repeatedly insisting that 'racing outside Italy is a waste of time', he was eventually persuaded to enter the 250 World Championship. This was despite Honda seeming unbeatable in the class, their riders having filled the first three places in the 1961 championship and taken first and second in 1962. But testing the water in two world championship races in 1962 gave Provini a second and a third place, and his new team-mate, Umberto Massetti, clinched second place at the Argentinian round.

So, for 1963, Morini squared up to Honda's four and world champion, Jim Redman. Though believing in the single's potential, the Morini team could not have been expecting success from the start, yet on 5 May, Morini won round one of the championship, the Spanish Grand Prix at Montjuic Park. Provini beat Redman's Honda four by 20sec, taking the track record in the process. Honda's predicted revenge failed to materialize when Morini won

Early 3½ with drum brakes (*see also* Segale).

A fine selection: 50cc overhead-valve Corsarini, 3½s of varying ages and a recent Granpasso.

the second round at Hockenheim, with Redman complaining that the Morini was much faster than his own bike. In practice for the French Grand Prix, Provini was once again fastest, and inside the track record, but torrential rain meant the race was cancelled.

Finances prevented Morini following the championship to the Isle of Man TT, and Provini could only manage third at Assen, behind winner Redman. From here on, Provini and Morini seemed forever on the back foot, especially when a strike and missing visas meant they could not even get to the East German round. Good news finally came at Monza, with Provini's win besting Redman's second place by almost 14sec. Alfonso Morini also lent a spare bike to a 21-year-old racer he felt had potential, giving Giacomo Agostini his world championship debut in the process.

Flushed with success and with the championship a real possibility, the Morini team made the expensive trip to Argentina. It nearly ended in disaster when Provini and Redman ran off-track, yet both managed to recover and make the podium a Morini–Honda one–two. Morini also took third with Massetti. Provini and Redman were now equal on points, and the championship would be decided at the final round at Suzuka on 10 November.

On the plane to Japan, Provini picked up severe earache, necessitating an operation while his team-mates struggled to get through customs. Although they made the start line, Provini could only claim fourth place, well

behind Redman's victorious Honda. So Jim Redman was world champion with just two points over Provini. In fairness, Redman was also competing in the 350cc and 125cc classes, but the resources of Honda versus Moto Morini did not bear comparison. So near, yet so far – yet so much to be proud of. Morini built the last four-stroke single to win a grand prix until Moto3 made them mandatory.

For 1964, Giacomo Agostini became Morini's number one rider, winning the Italian championship and claiming twelfth in the world championship, before making his move to MV Agusta. International competition became too much for Morini's scarce resources, although Dante Lambertini and Biavati continued experimenting with the single, including trying desmo heads. Much tweaking, including a shorter stroke and a 4-valve head, eventually produced 40bhp powering just 100kg (220lb) of dry weight. Not enough for the world stage, but sufficient to allow Morini a final Italian Championship with Angelo Bergamonti in 1967.

When Alfonso Morini died in 1969, many thought the firm would close, but it was instead reinvigorated by Morini's only daughter, Gabriella. She recruited Franco Lambertini (no relation to Dante) to design the seminal 3½ when he was just 25 years old and fresh from Ferrari. Franco Lambertini was the constant thread running through Moto Morini for some forty years, and is perhaps unique in designing complete motorcycles. He is also exceptional because, despite designing in excess of fifty engines for Morini, Piaggio, Gilera and Cagiva, he remains remarkably humble and genuinely surprised by the admiration he engenders in others. Quietly spoken, he does not come across as the typical Italian designer, and refers to himself simply as an 'artisan'.

When asked why he chose the then unfashionable V-twin layout for his first Morini, he replied:

It's very simple. The best engine for a bike is a V-twin. It is as narrow as a single, compact and good for a wide range of applications. This was important, given that I had no idea what types of motorcycle it might be required to power in the future. At the beginning, in 1971, when I conceived the first engine, the purpose was to produce an engine for the future. I was also always thinking about a modular engine, so we could use the same basic concept for different cylinder capacities and engine layouts. Only through modularity could the engine's life be kept long and its costs low, which they had to be given that production numbers were always going to be relatively small.

He was right: peak annual production never reached much more than 4,000 units during the 1970s and 1980s. The crankcases would also allow a single of 125cc to 250cc, an important option given how well Morini's earlier singles had sold, especially in the United States. The narrow 72-degree spacing of the 3½'s vee meant that using just a front cylinder on the crankcases would leave the cylinder leaning too far forward and break a visual link to the older models.

The 3½ project also intended to allow a capacity of up to 550cc, the only significant change being a doubling up of the crankshaft with an off set to counter vibration. Lambertini reminded people it was an idea Lancia put into production long before Honda did so with their VT500.

Lambertini was trialling a 67-degree, 720cc twin when Cagiva took over Morini. He also designed a 60-degree version for Gilera. Although Cagiva launched the beautiful Dart, a fully enclosed 350cc that Morini had taken to 400cc with bodywork from their 125 Freccia, it soon became clear that the acquisition was simply to mop up potential competition for Ducati. For a while it seemed

A rare (if unconvincing) 1980s restyling of the 3½.

The Dart, a 400cc version of the 3½ in Cagiva 125 Freccia bodywork, the first new model after the Cagiva takeover. TONY HARRISON

The latest Corsaro 1200ZZ. Morini boast that they very much source and build in Italy, almost unheard of in the modern motorcycle industry. MOTO MORINI

that Morini would wither on the vine and disappear.

But, by 1999, Cagiva had sold Ducati and its new owners were happy to sell the Moto Morini name to the Morini family, who still owned the engine manufacturer established by Franco Morini, Alfonso's nephew. Franco Lambertini was recruited to design a new engine and he delivered an 87-degree, V-twin, explaining that the negligible reduction from the perfect 90 degrees allowed the motor to be 25mm shorter than it otherwise would be. In 2004, the result was announced: the naked Corsaro 1200, followed by the 9½ road bike.

There was criticism of the 'snatchy' fuel-injection mapping in otherwise positive road tests. But the company folded in 2009, although a relaunch in 2012 hoped to succeed with a business model that involved only building motorcycles to order with no formal dealer network. It has not fared well, in the UK at least, although Morini continue to offer variations on the Corsaro theme. They are very proud of manufacturing in Italy with Italian components, which plays well with their domestic market, although inevitably it makes them expensive compared to those prepared to work with the Chinese. Even by Italian motorcycle standards, Morini fans are loyal, so it must be hoped that they can thrive despite – perhaps even because – Morini refuse to cut costs by diluting their Italian heritage.

MOTOBI – *SEE* BENELLI

MOTOM (1947–71)

Although unheard of in Britain, Motom were once the third-largest motorcycle maker in Italy, only outsold by Moto Guzzi and Garelli, although all were small fry compared to Lambretta and Vespa. Motom's success came from offering motorcycles and mopeds that seemed to take styling cues from the scooters, but Motom actually sprung from a car maker. Lancia's Battista Falchetto saw the success of lightweights, such as Ducati's Cucciolo and the Guzzino, and imagined a futuristic competitor with a car-style steel monocoque chassis. Lancia's access to funding and steel bodywork pressers Farina allowed for a new factory at Via Palma (Milan) with an efficient production line. Opting for a 48cc four-stroke engine to ensure reliability and economy, the first offering was the Motomic (intended to imply an atomic motorcycle), which, despite teething problems, convinced Motom's founders that they were on to something. But when they tried to move upmarket with the 160cc Delfino (dolphin) in 1952, sales were disappointing.

Motom 98. EL CAGANER

Motom Delfino (dolphin). MIDNIGHT BIRD

The Motom that really made the marque famous was the 1955, 98, another attempt to move from the moped market. Advertising spoke of its economic 98cc overhead-valve motor, but it was the styling that everybody talked about. The pressed steel bodywork did not just look like it was part of a sci-fi movie; it allowed fuel, steering and storage to be secured with a single turn of the key. Yet, as with all Motoms, it was great value for money, helped by a modern factory and large production runs. Like the Delfino, the 98 did not sell as well as expected and Motom retreated back into the moped market.

MOTO PIANA (1923–30)

This was the Florence-based workshop of Walter Piana. He offered mainly Villiers 250cc powered motorcycles, later using a side-valve vertical single 250cc of Piana's own design.

MOTO-REVE ITALIANA (1912–15)

Swiss Moto Reve built under licence with 300cc four-stroke singles and 497cc V-twins.

MOTORI MINARELLI – *SEE* FB MINARELLI

MOTOTECNICA DELL'ITALIA CENTRALE (1952–86)

Based near Florence these were sold under the Gabbiano (seagull) banner. Although the first models were 125cc two-strokes, the marque soon switched its focus to mopeds.

MOTO V (1927–31)

This was a 325cc single with stamped sheet metal frame, built by Vandone in Turin.

MT (1948–53)

Teresio Muratore's factory west of Milan in Tollengno offering a 250cc overhead-cam parallel twin with forward-slopping cylinders. Also sold as OMTs.

Moto Reve showing how early motorcycles were really bicycles with engines: not even a gearbox and still retaining pedals for starting and hills.

MÜLLER (1950–79)

Bruno Müller's Bologna factory initially used two- and four-stroke NSU engines from 49cc to 250cc. By the sixties, they briefly used Sachs and Villiers engines as they started to focus on the off-road market. Thereafter, Franco Morini engines were used from 50cc to 125cc, principally for off-road models plus sports mopeds.

MUSA (1947–49)

A Milan factory whose most popular model was the Musetta, powered by a 70cc motor with a three-speed gearbox.

MV AGUSTA (1946–)

Founding-father, Count Giovanni Agusta, designed his first aircraft in 1907 – a biplane tested in 1910 by towing it into the air with a car. Unable to fund development of an engine, Agusta turned to maintenance work, moving the family to Gallarate with premises at Cascina Costa between Malpensa (Milan) airport and Verghera. Agusta were also building aircraft for Regia Aeronautica and, in 1927, Agusta flew their first complete project – a monoplane – at the Milan show.

When Giovanni died in 1927, the company passed into the hands of his widow, Giuseppina, and young sons, Domenico, Vincenzo, Mario and Corrado. The business thrived, employing some 800 people and with workshops by the outbreak of the war. In 1943, Cascina Costa was occupied by German troops who remained in place until dispatched by the Allies.

Post-war, the eldest son Domenico – now Count Agusta – could not continue with his aviation business, so, like many others, turned to motorcycle manufacture. The Agusta family established Meccanica Verghera (MV) Agusta for the project in the hope that Giovanni Agusta's

Lucky charms are an Italian theme: Tazio Nuvolari had a tortoise-shaped piece of jewellery, an admirer gift to the fastest racer of a facsimile of the slowest animal.

The shape of MV fuel tanks gave them the *disco volante* (flying saucer) name.

company might one day return to aviation. The first MV prototype was a 98cc two-stroke intended to be known as the Vespa 98 until it was discovered that Piaggio had already registered Vespa as a trademark for their scooter. Italians often use insect names for two-strokes (such as the Garelli Mosquito) because of the similar noise they make, although Piaggio claimed it was because the rear bodywork of the scooter resembled a wasp's abdomen.

MV's early scooters and lightweights gave no hint of what was to come. With the 98 and its 125cc evolution proving successful in competition, Count Agusta could see that winning races brought him personal prestige and increased sales. In 1948, when Franco Bertoni rode one of the 125s to victory in the Italian Grand Prix at Monza, the Count decided to enter the inaugural world championship of 1949. But the 125 class was dominated by twin-cam Mondials, with the MV riders just ninth and tenth in the final standings.

MV were allowed to resume their aviation business in 1947 (initially with monoplanes and, from 1952, building Bell helicopters under licence), so they could afford to subsidize their racing. It also gave MV Agusta access to technology their competitors could only dream of, including a lubrication system that allowed them to offer a 100,000km warranty. But if the Count was to see his motorcycles beat Mondial, he would need proven motorcycle engineers as well. Between 1949 and 1950, he poached first Arturo Magni and then Piero Remor from Gilera, and set them to work (see also Gilera and Magni entries). Almost immediately, MV showed a 500cc four racer, remarkably similar to Gilera's, albeit with

improvements that would prove to be ill-advised, such as a shaft drive and torsion bar rear suspension. Even more brazenly, at the 1950 Milan show, MV exhibited a road-going version, the Turismo R19, claiming 38bhp and asking 950,000 lira – about three times the price of a decent 250cc. But only the show bike was ever built, as MV decided to focus on the 175cc road bikes, and Remor and Magni were asked to focus on developing a 125cc racing single alongside the big four.

For the 1950 500 World Championship, MV entered their Gilera clone with rider Arciso Artesiani, who had finished third the previous year with Gilera. But in the first five (of six) rounds he had only scored points at Spa Francorchamps, with a fifth-place finish. For the final round at the Grand Prix of Nations, held at Monza where the Count had a villa, two other riders were drafted in: Irishman Reg Armstrong was offered an upgrade from his Velocette single and Guido Leoni was also drafted into the team. Armstrong did not finish and, almost uniquely, would move from MV to Gilera. Leoni could only manage twelfth, so was out of the points. However, Artesiani came third, behind new champion, Umberto Massetti, on a Gilera and race winner, Geoff Duke, on a Norton. The sheer number of Nortons allowed them to finish joint winners with Gilera of the constructers' championship. MV Agusta was fourth, behind AJS. It is worth noting that over 120 riders competed in the 500 championship that year, albeit many solely at the Isle of Man TT.

The results were worse in the 125 class, however, with MV roundly thrashed by Mondial and rising star Moto Morini. MV's Felice Benasedo was placed joint-seventh

The 175 class was important enough to justify offering a twin-cam production racer.

The cam-drive gears as on the Benelli 250. Earles-style forks were surprisingly popular on Italian racing motorcycles.

at the end of the season in a field of only ten riders. The Count, infamous for his low moods and high expectations, cannot have been a happy man.

For 1951, Carlo Bandirola joined Artesiani on MV's 500s, the pair finishing the year twelfth and fourteenth in the championship, respectively, with MV garnering fifth in the constructors' title. In the 125 title chase, 1949 500cc champion Les Graham finished the year for MV in eighth, with team-mate Franco Bertoni twelfth.

1952 was the year the tide turned for MV. Les Graham finished runner-up on the 500cc, beating champion Umberto Massetti's Gilera to the win at the two final rounds, including at the Count's beloved Monza. And 1952 was the beginning of MV's thirty-eight riders' world championships, when Cecil Sandford brought home the 125 title. This also brought the first of MV's famous thirty-seven constructers' championships.

In the showrooms, the 1952 175 CSTL Turismo announced MV's arrival as a serious motorcycle manufacturer. This was the basis of the firm's overhead-valve and overhead-cam engines for many years, including the 250 Raid (colloquially 'long-distance racer'). The sportiest versions had a widely flared base to the fuel tank, gaining them the nickname 'disco volante' (flying saucer). Available with conventional front telescopic or Earles-type forks, the 175CSS was soon MV's best seller.

But 1953 proved disastrous in the 500 class with the incomparable Geoff Duke joining Gilera. He sorted the big four's wayward handling almost overnight, leading a clean sweep of the top three championship places for Gilera. Frustratingly, in the 125 class, MV took four of the top five spots, missing out to NSU for the top spot, who would repeat their success the following year.

MV's first 500 championship title came in 1956 when John Surtees controversially claimed the rider's title and MV's first constructors' win in the class. Duke had sided with privateers, asking for better money from the FIM who promptly handed him a lengthy ban that prevented him defending his title with Gilera. Reg Armstrong, also with Gilera, was similarly penalized.

Surtees could only manage third place for the Count in 1957, whose team had now collected five riders' titles: three 125s and one each in the 250 and 500 classes. There were also seven constructors' trophies: four in the 125 class, a brace for the 250s and one for the 500.

MV had a 500 six ready for 1958 when the Count was handed an open goal by his strongest competitors.

Count Agusta was either lucky or shrewd enough to focus on international races, rather than the Gran Fondo races, such as the Motogiro. In 1957, when Gran Fondos were banned and other Italian manufacturers withdrew from grand prix racing, the field was pretty much left

open to MV Agusta. The dominant marques – Gilera, FB Mondial, Moto Guzzi and MV Agusta – had made a pact to abandon the financially ruinous world championship, but MV reneged on the agreement. The other Italian factories' withdrawal would, however, allow newcomer Ducati the opportunity to enter international competition on less crowded grids.

With no real competition, the Count did not risk racing the six, and it would face competition just once. It was run at Monza in 1958 by John Hartle, who complained it had too narrow a power band for just five gears. MV revisited the concept when Honda and Mike Hailwood threatened their hegemony, testing a 350 six and being ready to build a 500 version; but when Honda walked away from racing at the end of 1967, they were again abandoned. In the end, MV won the 500 constructors' title every year from 1958 until 1973. They might have done the same with the 350 class but walked away from the class for a good chunk of the 1960s. Depending on who you ask, this was either because they feared being beaten by Honda (the 350 fours were effectively sleeved-down 500s, so a little heavy) or to make sure they could beat Honda in the 500 class. After 1960, MV also left the smaller classes to the rise of the Japanese.

When MV returned to the 350 class in 1966, it was with a much lighter triple. So successful was this that it was gradually developed into a 500. From 1966 to 1973, Agostini used the triple to win six 350 and seven 500 world championships. New team-mate Phil Read then used the triple to take the 1973 500 World Championship, but by now more power was needed. The 350 triple evolved into a 500 four but lost some of the sweet handling of the triple in the process, especially with the heavy 16-valve head.

It is often written that the MV racing department lost its influence with the Agusta family when Count Domenico died in 1971. In fact his successor, Count Corrado, brought in Giuseppe Bocchi from Ferrari to design a replacement for the racing fours. He designed and built a flat four 500 with liquid cooling and fuel injection. It was lighter, lower, more compact and much more powerful than the old inline four. Agostini and Read have both told me that the problem was trying to get Magni and Bocchi to cooperate, but there was a further complication.

Despite what is commonly believed, MV almost always had more power than their two-stroke rivals, but carried more weight, which affected acceleration and handling. It was the noise restrictions that the FIM imposed in 1976 that hurt MV and later Honda's NR500, because silencers robbed four-strokes of more power than they did two-strokes.

Yamaha's withdrawal from grand prix racing for 1976 left Agostini little choice but to set up a privateer team running old MV fours. Ironically, the old air-cooled fours had a significant advantage over the new Boxer for 1976 – the FIM allowed existing engines a year of grace, unfettered by the new noise limits. The new Boxer would have been required to run with silencers, robbing it of its power advantage over the old fours. So 1976 was always going to be the four-strokes' swansong in grand prix racing. With a new 350 four, Agostini dominated at Assen, where he beat Patrick Pons' TZ by 24sec. Agostini followed it up with a final win for MV, himself and the four-strokes at Germany's Nürburgring, beating run-

John Surtees 500cc four – the great man in black leathers is just visible.

ner-up Marco Lucchinelli's RG by almost a minute in the 500 race. It was enough for many in MV to press for the Boxer or a new liquid-cooled inline for 1977, but Count Corrado felt it would just be putting off the inevitable. Four stokes would not win again in grand prix racing until they were allowed almost double the capacity of two-strokes as the MotoGP era took over.

Despite all of their on-track exoticness, MV's road bikes never really caught much reflected glory. Pushrod singles were the norm, eventually relieved by the 1967 250B overhead-valve parallel twin. Despite twin carburettors, just 18bhp was initially claimed and, despite being of high quality, an equally high price meant sales were poor. A 350cc incarnation was more popular, revised in 1975 with more angular engine cases, a new frame and far sportier styling. This was the Ipotesi (hypothesis) – far from a bad motorcycle but just far more expensive than the superior Morini 3½, which itself was almost as expensive as a Japanese 750.

However, the 1960s had brought proof that people would pay a high price for a motorcycle in the shape of the BMW R69S. Twice the price of British competitors, the bike was sold as the ultimate tourer, shaft drive and all. Put the MV 600, first shown in 1965, against the BMW and you wonder if it inspired the Count to sell his first four. And by 1970, specialists were proving that high prices would also be paid for effective sporting motorcycles and MV responded with

Even John Surtees needs a reminder of how many gears are available and what shift pattern is used.

the 750 Sport. The penultimate four was the 1975 America, enlarged to 789cc with new bodywork.

The final MV four was the Boxer, the name swiftly changed to Monza at Ferrari's behest, as they had been using the nomenclature for their Berlinetta Boxer. The Boxer/Monza was taken out to 837cc, and incorporated new camshafts and larger carburettors. Cast-alloy wheels became standard fitments, and a new look was designed for the machine. The new machine was faster than the America by approximately 10mph, giving it a top speed in the region of 145mph (233km/h).

The round case 350cc was a simple pushrod twin and not really competition for the equivalent Ducati or Morini.
MYKEL NICOLAOU

The later 350 Ipotesi (hypothesis) had a boxier style to the engine cases and a much improved frame.

The company won their last grand prix in 1976, and by the end of the season they were out of racing. The company's precarious economic position forced MV Agusta into the arms of government finance department EFIM (Ente Partecipazioni e Finanziamento Industria Manifatturiera), which dithered between folding MV and allowing it to absorb Ducati, for which the EFIM were also responsible. MV hobbled on to 1980, thankfully without taking Ducati with them.

Cagiva purchased the MV Agusta rights in 1991 – a little surprising given that they were still in the throes of trying to rebuild Ducati, with the 916 and Monster still a few years off. Perhaps it was because Claudio Castiglioni had Massimo Tamburini under his wing, and Tamburini never made any secret of his belief that inline fours were the ultimate sports motorcycle power plant.

Ferrari were apparently more than happy to help with the engine design, which, for reasons of historical association, Castiglioni wanted to launch as a 750cc. Engine design team leader, Andrea Goggi, had worked on Cagiva's grand prix effort, as well as at Ducati. While admitting that the Suzuki GSX-R had been taken as a starting point, working with Ferrari quickly led to little beyond the overall layout being shared. The idea of boring cylinders at slightly different angles – in effect creating an ultra-narrow V4 – was dismissed as complicating production for a negligible reduction in size. Goggi worked closely with the chassis team, both ruling out inlets at the front with rear-facing exhausts as being impossible to

package. But Ferrari's radial 4-valve head made full production, as did downdraft fuel-injection tracts.

The early prototypes had a rather boxy bodywork, and constant delays meant that a cynical press doubted that the new MV Agusta's would make production. Those cynics did not know Castiglioni or that the delays were due to the Italian Government changing terms on the loans that had allowed Castiglioni to save Ducati. In the end Castiglioni bit the bullet, sold Ducati and pressed on with the MV project. In 1996, the Texas Pacific Group (TPG) bought 51 per cent of Ducati for 500 billion lire – about $325 million. Castiglioni had bought Ducati for $5 million in 1985.

Castiglioni also took Tamburini to MV, along with Monster designer Miguel Galluzzi to Cagiva, causing some in the business sector who understood Ducati to wonder what TPG had paid for. The new Ducati 998 engine had been promised with new styling, which, rumour had it, Tamburini transferred to the MV. So TPG launched the 998 – a much updated engine and not just an increase in capacity – with rather bland new graphics, the only visual change from the 916/996. The MV's four underseat silencers echoed the 916 design but, apparently affronted by BMW lifting the look for the R1100S, Castiglioni patented the MV's design.

The MV Agusta F4 was finally shown to the public in 1998, and launched to the press at Monza in spring of the following year. There were still plenty of Doubting Thomases, but not about the styling: I owned a 998 at

The collectors dream: a 750cc aka the Sport.

the time and felt I had been robbed. Monza is a phenomenally fast circuit that sucks the sense of true speed from riders in a potentially lethal way. But Claudio Castiglioni wanted the historic link to Count Agusta, despite one journalist complaining that the indicated 165mph (265km/h) could only be down to a fibbing speedometer. A radar gun was found and the journalist spent the rest of the launch apologizing. The only other criticism of the new model was the occasionally hesitant fuel-injection, but that was typical of even Japanese motorcycles' fuel-injection at the time.

Castiglioni was a marketing genius. The first F4s were exotic limited editions with gold anodizing on some components to link to the genuine magnesium alloy parts, which included the wheels and swinging arm. 200 were initially promised, and then 300, outrageously priced unless you were famous and likely to ride one, like Ayrton Senna. People like that got a free motorcycle.

Perhaps the only trick Castiglioni missed was making the MV F4 a 750. He could have linked to the 850 Boxer and been closer in performance to motorcycles such as the Fireblade. But he and Tamburini stuck to their agreed Motorcycle Art tag and even parts that cannot be seen without dismantling an MV, are still beautiful today.

The next part of MV's history involved Castiglioni selling it to a Far East conglomerate, then buying it back for next to nothing. He did the same with Harley-Davidson in 2008 (who had already owned the factory in its Aermacchi years), selling them MV and then allowing them to spend millions developing new models. Harley-Davidson thought owning a sports bike manufacturer would diversify their business, but the 2008 financial crash left them with little choice than to sell MV back to Castiglio-

Cagiva had a run of 500cc triple replicas built as soon as they bought MV Agusta. This is Agostini's.

ni for 1 euro in 2010. Shortly thereafter, MV announced a 600 triple, developed with Harley cash, to give Castiglioni the two engine layouts most associated with Count Agusta's racing stable.

MV Agusta's motorcycles are expensive, but not compared to the original fours or Tamburini's Bimotas. They are built at Varese rather than Verghera, but it is not far

Much revised bodywork would be followed by an 850cc version.

Kay's build these 3-cylinder replicas for racing, but they are expensive.

Michael Dunlop and Kay's MV 500 triple ready for the Senior Classic TT.

The 750 F4 was the start of Cagiva's MV Agusta revival.

away, and it is the old Aermacchi factory after all. Without Claudio Castiglioni's touch (he died in 2011, aged 64), MV has struggled, tying their fortunes to Mercedes via the AMG brand. But even this Ducati fanatic would consider that modern MVs have always been far better detailed than anything that ever came out of Bologna. Or, indeed, anywhere else.

MVB (1954–56)

Based in Milan, they built mopeds and lightweights with bought-in 48cc, 125cc and 147cc two-stroke engines.

NAGAS & RAY – *SEE* JONGHI

NAVONE – *SEE* BAUDO

NAZZARO (1926–28)

Eugenio Nazzaro's workshops in Turin offered motorcycles with his own overhead-valve 175cc motor and separate three-speed gearbox.

NB (1930–39)

Nicola Bordone in Milan originally offered tricycles with 250cc and 500cc engines with a shaft drive. When he started making motorcycles in 1938, he changed the marque name to NB. There is some evidence that the three-wheelers, and possibly motorcycles, were again offered post-war until around 1957. These used an overhead-cam version of the 500cc, ultimately taken to 600cc.

NCR (1967–

Giorgio Nepoti, Rino Caracchi and Luigi Rizzi initially were a car and motorcycle repair workshop. When they moved into race preparation, and Rizzi left, the final R was changed to stand for racing. NCR were incredibly supportive of Ducati's racing efforts, although their part in race preparation was always overstated by Fabio Taglioni to prevent his government paymasters realizing he was spending money going racing when it was strictly forbidden. NCR did not build any 900 F1s, one of which Mike Hailwood used to win the 1978 Formula 1 TT, despite Ducati's catalogue of the year claiming that to be the case. However, there is little doubt that their workmanship was superb, radially drilling the disc brakes on Ducati's endurance racers to aid cooling and saving weight. Although the NCR name has had nothing to do with its founders for many years, the business still very much ex-

Rino Caracchi (the C in NCR, closest to the camera) shows off part of his motorcycle collection. In the jacket, raising a camera, is Pat Slinn, who was a Ducati mechanic for Mike Hailwood and Tony Rutter.

ists, producing special parts and modified Ducatis that are very much in that proud tradition.

NENCIONI (1926–28)

A motorcycle with a 125cc Della Ferrera twin-cylinder, two-stroke engine built by Carlo Nencioni near Florence.

NETTUNIA – *SEE* BUSI

NIBBIO (1946–52)

The first Italian scooter used a 98cc two-stroke engine with a tubular chassis. Built initially by Gianca di Monza, from 1949 production passed to the San Cristoforo of Milan. They also offered a disc-valve, two-stroke 125cc, which was updated in 1952 and subsequently sold as the Simonetta.

OVARA (1930–35)

Angelo Novara built motorcycles with 125cc JAP and Chaise engines in Legnano.

OASA – SEE ALIPRANDI

OCMA – SEE DEVIL

OLIVA (1920–25)

A factory on the coast west of Genoa at Vado Ligure, they used the 175 Train engine with a separate two-speed gearbox.

OLIVERIO (1929–32)

A Turin-based factory that used overhead-valve Sturmey–Archer engines of 350cc and 500cc.

OLLEARO (1921–53)

Naphtali Ollearo's Turin workshop started out repairing bicycles and later motorcycles, and is probably most famous for its four-wheeled products, building short-run variations for Fiat. But before that there were two-stroke powered motorcycles of 125cc, 131cc and 175cc. During the 1930s, the range expanded to include overhead-valve 175s and 350s (the Sirena): there was also an overhead-cam 500cc (the Perla) and a racing 250cc. These four-strokes all had shaft drive, a first in Italy, bar the 1923 Garabello four. This made them ideal to adapt for three-wheel use, but also the most expensive motorcycles on the market. But then they were marketed as 'the first motorcycles of the future'. Post-war, the 150cc and 175cc included a 'lady' version with leg shields, scooters and auxiliary motors.

OLYMPIA (1951–54)

A Borghi factory (inland from Rimini) that was principally a bicycle factory, but also produced two-stroke mopeds and 125s.

OMA (1952–55)

Officine Meccaniche Amadori was based in Bologna and offered an overhead-valve 175cc with a three-speed gearbox.

OMB (1932–34)

Officine Meccaniche Broglia was founded by Angelo Blatto after leaving Ladetto. They produced single-cylinder race bikes from 175cc to 500cc.

OME (1920–21)

An electric motorcycle built by Ernest Giordani, running either 6V or 12V Tudor batteries to produce 250W. Despite weighing 100kg (220lb) it could reach 15mph (25kph).

OMEA (1950–53)

A two-stroke 125cc with a three-speed gearbox, designed by Carlo Bottari and built in Milan.

OMN (1924–25)

A lightweight built in Navarre with Villiers of 147cc and 172cc two-stroke engines.

OPRA – SEE GILERA

OR (1928–31)

Italian motorized bicycles presented in 1928 by the Officine Riunite di Costruzioni Meccaniche of Milan. Side- and overhead-valve 175s.

ORAM (1949–52)

Officina Reconstruzione Automobili e Motocicli, offering a 125cc built in Bologna.

ORESTE & GARANZINI – *SEE* GARANZINI AND MG

ORIONE (1923–28)

Guido Carpi of Milan specialized in the production of sporting two-stroke engines, the 125cc and 175cc especially. Also produced clip-on motors for bicycles.

ORIX – *SEE* PRINA

OTTINO (1926–35)

Founded in Turin by the Ottino brothers, they produced motorcycles powered by a 125cc Della Ferrera or 175cc JAP motors.

OTTOLENGHI (1928–32)

Motorcycles built in Caluso, north-east of Turin by Ottolenghi and Actis. Initially, they used 346cc Piazza or Ladetto & Blatto 173cc and 346cc engines. JAP motors were also used from 1930.

PANDA (1980–85)

Off-road light bikes with 79cc Sachs and 125cc Franco Morini engines.

PARILLA (1946–67)

Giovanni Parrilla was born in Spain in 1912, but his family moved to Calabria in southern Italy around 1920. By the time Parrilla was a teenager it was clear he was fascinated by things mechanical in general, and motorcycles in particular. After a spell in the military, he became a mechanic with a spark plug franchise in Milan. Parrilla apparently spent much of his time bemoaning Italy's inability to build a racing motorcycle to beat the dominant British. The story is that Parrilla's frustration finally boiled over into a hubristic boast that he could build a better race bike than any of the existing Italian factories. In the heat of the moment, a bet was sealed and Parrilla set to work.

This was 1946, when the most admired racing motorcycle was the Manx Norton. With perfect logic, Parrilla bought one, took it apart (carefully measuring and note-taking as he went) and reassembled it; then sold it on to fund development of his own version.

Fairy tales do come true. Parrilla's first Parilla (he apparently thought dropping the second r made the name seem more Italian) won its debut race. Despite demand, Parrilla refused to sell this first bike, and a production line was born. The design was actually by Giuseppe Salmaggi (of Gilera Saturno and Moto Rumi racing twin

Parilla was named after a Spaniard who spelt his name Parilla and had an Italian greyhound as a trademark.

The early 250cc racer.

An MDDS 175cc.

fame) guided by Parrilla's demands. Like Norton, Parrilla specified a bevel-drive single overhead cam with hairpin valve springs, although his motorcycle was just 250cc, reflecting the Italian market's appetite for smaller displacement engines.

That first race was at Lecco, on Moto Guzzi's doorstep, at a time when Guzzi were Italy's largest motorcycle manufacturer. The production 250cc was launched at the Milan show in 1947 with huge 10.2in brakes, as seen on the racer (8in or less might have been expected), leading to the nickname '*padellone*' (frying pans). Two were bought by German racer Roland Schnell who, with friend Hermann Gablenz, created a twin-cam 350cc version. During 1951, Schnell won two international races at Madrid and Schaffhausen (in Switzerland), as well as winning the German Championship with the bike.

After such a flying start, Parrilla's next bike seemed like one step backwards. In fact, the 1952 Fox was truly inspired, although the bare bones of the specification (175cc, overhead valves) made it seem no more than an equal for its many competitors. The clever bit was a tower on the left-hand crankcase, covering a chain driving a high camshaft (*camme rialzata*) by the cylinder head. The cam ran two incredibly short pushrods acting on 90-degree included-angle valves. The design offered much of the advantages of an overhead-cam engine, but with simple valve adjustment and a compact cylinder head, permitting a similarly compact and sturdy frame. The bottom end was just as clever, with a built-up crankshaft and caged roller big end, with helical gear drive to a four-speed gearbox. Again, designed by Salmaggi, this

time working with Alfredo Bianchi, the unique layout remained competitive for more than a decade and continued in production until Parrilla motorcycles closed in 1967. Limited editions were made for racing, and one was used in 125cc, 250cc and '350' (actually 256cc) to race across Europe in 1964. These included world championship rounds with Rider Richard Morley, who would become managing director at Lotus.

The greatest success was the 250 Wildcat off-road versions that meant perhaps 80 per cent of Parrilla's production went to the US. Ironically, it was the genius of the Parrilla's compact layout that killed it – the cam tower meant 250cc was the absolute maximum capacity and Parrilla couldn't fund production of the larger crankcases that would have allowed enlargement and a five-speed gearbox. A 350cc twin had been shown in 1952, but only a handful was built.

Parrilla diversified into two-strokes, the most remarkable being the Slughi (Desert Greyhound) of 1957. It was available with either a 125cc two-stroke or 99cc and 125cc overhead-valve engines. While Parrilla had high hopes for the Slughi, sales were disappointing and production ceased in 1964. In the United States they were sold as the Ramjet or Ramjet Streamliner.

Parrilla diversified into two-stroke engines and racing go-kart manufacturing, which survives today because Giovani Parrilla was forced by his banks to choose between these highly profitable markets and motorcycling. Yet the motorcycles were of astounding quality, especially considering what a small concern Moto Parilla was, and deserve to be better known.

Parilla did not just offer sports bikes, there was a range of lightweights and engines built for others, including Go Karts.

SLUGHI 99 completo di paragambe
SLUGHI 99 leg shields complete

SLUGHI 99 - tipo America
SLUGHI 99 - america type

John Crooks MDDS 175cc was a winner of *Classic Bike* magazine's restoration of the year.

Note drive to a high cam allowing very short pushrods and so more precise valve control.

PATON (1957–)

When the big Italian factories agreed to leave racing at the end of 1957, Mondial's chief mechanic, Giuseppe Pattoni (Peppino or Pep to friends), and designer, Lino Tonti, set up shop with a pile of spare parts and hopes of continuing to race under another name.

Their first design was a twin-cam 125cc dubbed Mondial-Paton (PAttoni TONti) but Mondial's owners, the Bosellis, insisted they drop the Mondial name, so that it did not appear that the pact with other factories to cease racing had been broken in any way. One of the first customers for the new bike was Stan Hailwood, despite already having an MV Agusta 125, for his son's Isle of Man TT debut. But after practice, Mike decided to race the Paton, taking it to seventh place, only beaten by works machines from MV, Ducati and MZ.

Despite the 125's promise and comparative sales success, Tonti left Pattoni to his own devices in 1959 to take up a position with Bianchi. Pattoni pushed ahead with a 247cc parallel twin, effectively doubling up the 125. The twin was first raced at Modena in 1964 with Gian Piero Zubani and, like the 125, proved to be fast and reliable. A few months later, Alberto Pagani took the bike to third place in the lightweight (250cc) TT, in a race where only eight of the sixty-four starters completed all six laps. In the process he averaged over 86mph (138km/h) for 226

miles (364km), still over 10mph slower than winner Jim Redman's Honda and Alan Shepherd's MZ. But those were not motorcycles that could be bought, whereas the Paton was very much for sale. It was also, compared to other privateer options, the fastest bike on the Highlander straight at 124mph (200km/h).

In 1966, infamous Ducati importer Bill Hannah – he bought a shipment from the US importers and undercut Vic Camp, who was effectively Ducati UK – joined forces with Paton, his funding allowing further development. Over the following two years, the twin, recognized as Pattoni's masterpiece, grew to 350cc and finally to 500cc. In 1967, Angelo Bergamonti took the Italian senior championship with a Paton, beating Agostini and his MV Agusta. There were also podiums in several world championship races and Billie Nelson finished fourth in the 1969 500 World Championship aboard a Paton.

In 1968, 4-valve heads were first tried, becoming standard by 1970 and raising power from 65bhp to 70bhp. But, in 1970, Hannah withdrew his financial support and Pattoni was again on his own, often with just one mechanic. He recruited Roberto Gallina, who finished a creditable third in the Yugoslavian Grand Prix, only beaten by Agostini and Angelo Bergamonti's MVs. Despite only entering four rounds, Gallina finished the year eleventh. Billie Nelson was sixteenth from three entries on his Paton the following year, with Gallina unable to finish either of the rounds he entered. And, despite a new Bimota frame, by

Ollie Linsdale in the winner's enclosure after victory in the Senior Classic TT aboard his Paton 500cc twin.

1974, it was clear that four-strokes would no longer be competitive against the two-strokes, and Pattoni started on a completely new engine.

Italy was ruling the 250 class by now with the Harley-Davidson – Aermacchi two-stroke twins being developed by Sandro Colombo and ridden by Walter Villa. Based upon these HD RR250 motors, the 1975 Paton was a 90-degree V4 two-stroke – a first in grand prix racing – but, despite help from his son Roberto and Virginio Ferrari, Pattoni struggled. Eventually he realized Paton needed to withdraw from racing to focus on development. By the early 1980, with help from Cagiva's motocross programme, their cylinder heads especially, and Walter Villa's stint as test rider, genuine progress was being made. Villa's name drew publicity and, in 1983, Frenchman Eric Saul raced for the team bringing valuable sponsorship. If passion and commitment won races, Paton would have been world champions, but not against the Japanese factories' research and development departments. By 1985, the engine was effectively a pair of stacked 250cc parallel twins, giving 120bhp – impressive, given Paton's resources, and enough to win the 1988 European Championship with Vittorio Scatola. Up on the world stage, Paton just did not have the resources to be competitive, and by now Pattoni was clearly racing for love rather than any hope of serious success.

In 1997, racing having become more about money and especially television rights, Paton was refused automatic registration for the world championship after thirty-nine years of participation. This was not enough to stop the Paton team, who accepted they would only compete occasionally as a 'wild card' – a dream that continued until 30 August 1999, when Giuseppe Pattoni succumbed to a fatal heart attack after a test session.

Roberto Pattoni continued to chase his father's dream, helped by Cagiva sharing their lessons from some remarkable grand prix achievements. But the arrival of four-strokes and MotoGP finally brought Paton's racing to an end. Or it might have done, without some exceptional developments on the Isle of Man.

After Roberto Pattoni shut down the two-stroke project in 2002, he remembered that his father's 500cc twin had been built to beat the British singles that had dominated the world championship fifty years earlier, and that the same would hold true in modern classic racing. In 2004, the factory swung back into action and, in 2007, won their first Isle of Man race with Ryan Farquhar at the Manx.

For the 2007 Tourist Trophy centenary, Steve Linsdell decided to race a 2001 Paton two-stroke in the centenary Senior TT – a brave decision given the competition were

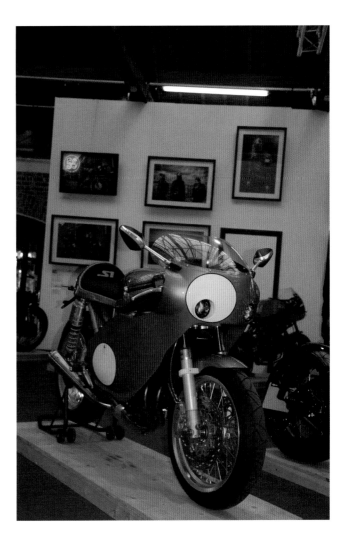

Patton also offer a Kawasaki-powered version of their motorcycle, drastically cutting the price and allowing homologation for road use.

on 1000cc four-strokes. Sadly, the bike only lasted half-race distance, although that is still further than any modern grand prix is run for. Steve had run a Paton 500cc four-stroke twin in the previous year's Manx Grand Prix, finishing second in the Classic Senior.

Josh Brookes won again for Paton at the 2017 Senior Classic TT, his bike proving more reliable than the Kay replica MV triples. And not only is the Paton considerably cheaper than the MV, it is built in the same factory that its forefathers came from. It is a continuation, rather than a replica. And for those who cannot afford the admittedly steep price that a hand-built racing motorcycle has to cost, or prefer to ride on the road, there is also a road-legal version powered by a Kawasaki twin. It is hard to think of another man, effectively working alone and only followed by his son, that has achieved as much in the motorcycle world as Giuseppe Pattoni.

PATRIARCA (1907–33 / 1951)

Originally, 100cc single-cylinder, two-stroke engines, built in Turin for Gustavo Patriarca, to power bicycles. From 1924 the complete motorcycle used Moser and JAP motors of 125cc, 175cc and 250cc, switching in 1930 to engines built in-house. Closing in 1933, post-war Patriarca attempted an unsuccessful relaunch with a four-stroke vertical single of 248cc.

PERUGINA (1953–62)

Based in Castel del Piano in Perugia, they produced two- and four-stroke motorcycles of 160cc, 175cc and 250cc. The owner, Giuseppe Menicucci, had begun producing motorcycles in 1930, first under the Menicucci banner, then BMP (see BMP) and finally with Perugina.

PG (1929–30)

Parasacco and Guarino of Turin built perhaps a handful of overhead-valve 175s. There was also a Giuseppe Parena around the same time, offering 124cc clip-on engines under the PG banner.

PIAZZA (1924–37)

Antonio Piazza of Turin offered motorcycles with ei-ther a 125cc two-stroke or an overhead-valve 175cc engine. Between 1926 and 1928, most production was of engines for other factories, and thereafter focus was on the 175cc motorcycles, now also offered with a side-valve option.

PIOLA (1919–21)

Gianni Pio e Figli (and sons) also known as PFG, offered a side-valve, 620cc flat twin.

PIOVATICCI (1973–75)

Pesaro furniture manufacturer, Egidio Piovaticci, originally only sponsored local road-racer, Eugenio Lazzarini, and the first 'Piovaticci' was simply a rebranded Maico 125. There was then a 250cc version, but neither machine brought success.

Presumably inspired by neighbour Morbidelli, Piovaticci commissioned Jan Thiel and Martin Mijwaart (who had been developing racing two-strokes in the Netherlands under the Jamathi banner) to develop completely new 50cc and 125cc Piovaticcis. These were extremely successful but, by the end of 1975, the project had bankrupted Egidio Piovaticci, who lost not only his motorcycles but also his furniture business. The project went to Bultaco, who also retained Thiel and Mijwaart and went on to use what they had learned to win six world championships with Ángel Nieto.

PIROTTA (1947–58)

Principally, a moped and clip-on engine manufacturer based in Gorgonzola (where the cheese comes from), east of Milan. But there were at least two motorcycles sold as Lusso Sport, both with two-stroke engines. The 75cc model was conventional enough but, with pedals and an automatic clutch, was in essence a large moped. However, the 1954 160cc had a four-speed gearbox and a steel tank that swept around the forks to support the headlight.

PIUMA (1989–92)

Off-road motorcycles using Husqvarna four-stroke engines.

PIVA (1922–24)

Milan-built, with 110cc two-stroke engines.

PL (1927)

Based in Tolentino, south of Pesaro, they offered lightweights with two-stroke engines of 49cc, 98cc and 132cc.

PO (1921–23)

Motorcycles offered by Pagni and Occhialini of Florence, all with a 347cc, two-stroke, single engine.

POLET (1923–24)

Achille Polet's Milan workshop offered motorcycles powered by an inlet over exhaust, 481cc single engine.

POSDAM (1926–30)

The Turin workshop of the Possio brothers offered inlet over exhaust engines of 123cc, 150cc and 173cc.

PR (1935–36)

Pietro Rosati of Turin built overhead-cam, 500cc singles.

PREMOLI (1935–38)

A small factory in Varese used Python and OMB 498cc singles. They also offered a limited series of racing motorcycles with overhead-valve, 175cc engines.

PRINA (1949–54)

Based in Alessandria, south-west of Milan, they principally manufactured scooters, including the Orix brand, but did offer two-stroke powered 125cc and 175cc sports motorcycles. There was also a motorcycle with a 175cc ILO two-stroke motor.

PRINETTI & STUCCHI/ STUCCHI (1883–1926)

Originally manufactured sewing machines and bicycles in Milan. It was owned by engineers and politicians, Augusto Stucchi and Giulio Prinetti. Their first motorized tricycles and quadracycles were designed and built by Ettore Bugatti using two De Dion engines and a Rochet–Schneider frame. By the turn of the century, they were building some 7,000 vehicles a year.

In 1901, the company was named Stucchi e Compagni (Stucchi and Company) when Prinetti left to become Italian Minister of Foreign Affairs, which gave Ettore Bugatti cause to emigrate to France, where he established the Bugatti car marque.

The Stucchi motorcycle was a four-stroke, single-cylinder, 500cc with inlet over exhaust valves. In 1905, V-twins followed. During the war, Adalberto Garelli ran the company and added 750cc and 1000cc V-twins to the range. After he left in 1919 to establish his eponymous motorcycle factory, the 1000cc V-twin was updated and a 350 Blackburne side-valve model was offered. A 550cc Blackburne engine and two-cylinder 1000cc JAP V-twins followed in the final year of production.

QUAGLIOTTI (1902–07)

Carlo Quagliotti's Turin factory was one of the leading motoring pioneers. Initially an engine builder, from 1904 he was offering motorcycles with 2bhp Peugeot engines. Cars followed and later motorcycles with singles and V-twin engines from Aster and De Dion–Bouton.

RANZANI (1925–31)

A Milan marque that used mainly four-stroke German Heros engines, although some were fitted with 170cc overhead-valve Norman English engines.

RAS – *SEE* FUSI

REITER (1927–29)

Based in Turin, they used 250cc and 350cc Blackburne engines with side- and overhead-valve options.

RIGAT (1912–15)

Luigi Rigat built motorcycles in Milan. Originally, they used their own 487cc engines, but, in 1914, switched to the German side-valve 499cc Fafnir motor.

ROMERO (1934–36)

Side-valve, horizontal 500cc singles built in Turin.

RONDINE

There were four companies using the Rondine (swallow) banner, all close to Milan:
(1923–28)
Based in Melegnano, they used 98cc Train engines.
(1951–54)
Based in Pavia, they used 124cc and 147cc two-stroke Sachs engines.
(1968–73)
Based in Vigevano, the project of ex-racer Alfredo Copeta, they offered off-road and racing 50s.
See Gilera for the 4-cylinder racer.

ROSSELLI (1899–10)

Based in Turin and originally known as Rosselli & Castellazzi. Production included Lilliput engines for bicycles, Optimus engines for boats and cars, and motorcycles with engines rated between 1bhp and 5bhp, including a 2.5bhp, 258cc power unit. The Rosselli was a 'ladies' model with a 1.75bhp engine and netting to prevent a rider's skirt getting caught in moving parts.

ROSSI (1929)

Based in Varese and unique in Italy at the time for using aluminium alloy frame and transverse 90-degree, V-twin, overhead-valve, 346cc or 480cc engines.

ROSSI (1950–55)

Off-road motorcycles built in Parma, initially with 125cc and 175cc ILO engines, but later making their own two-strokes.

ROTA (1950–54)

Designed and built by Felice Rota in Biella, west of Milan, with an overhead-valve, 500cc engine and a four-speed gearbox fitted to touring, sport and racing models.

ROVETTA (1900–06)

Giovanni Rovetta, based in Brescia, was an early proponent of water-cooling, which featured on his first 2.5bhp engine. Later he offered a complete machine with an air-cooled single.

Rubinelli, probably early 1920s, with a 142cc or 172cc motor that also powered some Gaia models.

ROYAL (1923–28)

Founded by Fratelli Santogostino in Milan, who initially offered 132cc two-strokes, and then 346cc and 498cc models, using JAP and Blackburne engines. With his brother he offered a version of the 132 as the Super Royal.

RUBINELLI (1921–28)

Icaro Rubinelli was initially based in Stresa, on Lake Maggiore, and later moved to Milan. He offered 122cc and 172cc two-stroke models, but also sold engines alone, notably to Gaia.

RUMI (1949–62)

Originally a foundry and machinery manufacturer based in Bergamo, north-east of Milan. During the Second World War, Rumi produced two-man submarines and also torpedoes and, like Agusta and Aermacchi, turned to motorcycles post-war. Owner Donnino Rumi was an artist and a sculptor, so was never going to produce a motorcycle like anybody else's.

The first Rumi prototype, the Amisia, was almost identical to the first production models, apart from dropping the rotary valve in favour of cheaper piston porting. The 124.77cc horizontal twin could be supplied with a three- or four-speed gearbox and featured leading link front forks that would feature on almost

Rumi racer with Maserati moped in the foreground.

Early 125cc with plunger
rear suspension.

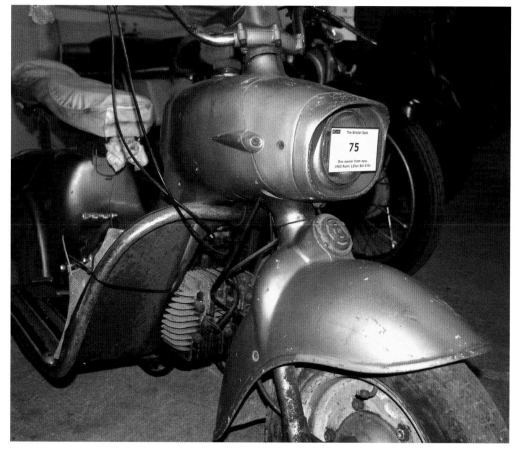

The Forminchino (little
ant) in the original
Bol d'Or gold paint
but probably ripe for
restoration.

all Rumis, although telescopic forks were sometimes an option. There was a racing version from 1951 until 1955 – the first model being the Competizione SS52 Gobbetto. This retained the standard models' plunger rear suspension and, from 1953, an integral fairing and fuel tank.

Rumi's designer was Giuseppe Salmaggi who had penned the Gilera Saturno and had worked with FN and Parilla. Even the standard models could comfortably exceed 70mph (113km/h) and, with the twin 23mm Del Orto carburettor option, touch 90mph (145km/h). Rumi won the team prize in the inaugural 1953 Motogiro, with best-placed rider Rochei finishing fourth overall. In the 1955 Milano-Taranto, Pietro Carissoni took another fourth place in the 125 class, with four of the top ten class finishers being aboard Rumis.

At this point, Rumi seemed to lose direction. In 1952, Salmaggi showed a proposed 250cc grand prix racer, a parallel twin with cylinders inclined forward by 27 degrees. Twin overhead-cams were gear-driven, and final drive was by shaft. It went well enough in testing to gain MV Agusta's attention, but was never run again. Mick Walker speculated that perhaps it was deemed too heavy or was unreliable: readers may wonder how such a machine might promote sales of the 125cc two-stroke twins, or if Salmaggi was getting Rumi to pay for his very expensive business card.

Salmaggi then showed a new racing engine that did bear a resemblance to the road-going Rumi's motor. It was just that the 125cc racing horizontal twin was a four-stroke, with Ducati-like bevel-driven twin cams. Again, the engine appeared at a few shows before disappearing.

Rumi's marketing department had noticed that scooters were outselling motorcycles by a huge margin. Rumi's engine lent itself to a scooter layout, and would be more stable than a conventional scooter with the engine just behind the front wheel, rather than hanging off the rear one. The logic was that 14in wheels would give motorcycle-like handling, and the result was what we would now call a big-wheel scooter – the Scoiattolo (squirrel).

At this point, Donnino Rumi rolled his sleeves up to produce what would be the most successful Rumi of all. Having seen the success of scooters, he sculpted his 'little ant' (Formichino) around the 125cc two-stroke motor, detuned to make it more flexible. Although the Formichino was expensive because of the cast aluminium alloy components, this was quickly followed by an economy version – the E – using steel.

In 1955, the Bol d'Or 24h race introduced a scooter class, for which the Formichino was ideally suited. With its motorcycle-style weight distribution and the two-stroke twins' racing heritage, Rumi won the scooter class three years on the trot from 1958. Riders Foidelli and Bois were sixteenth overall but first in the 125 scooter

The V-twins were planned and advertised but never made production.

class, covering 1,302 miles (2,096km) at an average of 54mph (87km/h). The winning Triumph 500 managed 1,632 miles (2,626km) at 68mph (109km/h).

Rumi celebrated with a gold-painted Formichino (Bol d'Or means gold bowl) on the motorcycle front. Rumi's trademark engine was taken to 200cc for the Granturismo with a big seat and integral fairing and fuel tank, similar to the second series Gobbetto.

In 1960, Rumi showed an ambitious longitudinal four-stroke V-twin, with cylinder finning shared between the front and rear heads and barrels. It was to be built in 98cc, 125cc and 175cc capacities, both for a new range of motorcycles and a conventional-looking scooter. They never passed the prototype stage and were probably what

bankrupted Rumi. Their products were often hailed as best in class by the press, but the public never seemed to agree in sufficient numbers. The Rumi name reappeared on a few racing motorcycles in the 1990s but, other than that, it seems to have gone forever.

RUSPA (1925–29)

Luigi and Franco Ruspa's Turin workshop, first offered a 124cc two-stroke and then an overhead-valve 175cc. In 1928, it became Ruspa & Gaeta, and an overhead-cam 350cc was added to the range.

S4 (1939–54)

Sergio Secondo built racing bikes with the help of Ercole Beltritti and Alfredo Berola. The air-cooled 350cc and 500cc 4-cylinder, transverse engines with double overhead-camshafts achieved some success post-war, and were years ahead of their time.

SAETTA (1932–41)

Brothers Mario and Riccardo Bertolo, with their brother-in-law Mario Bertot, had a car-repair shop in Forno Canavese, north-west of Turin. They offered one motorcycle under the Saetta (arrow) banner, with an overhead-valve, 500cc JAP engine and a four-speed Burman gearbox.

SALVE (1925–26)

These were motorcycles built in 1925 by the Società Automotociclette Lombardo Veneto-Emilia of Milan. The engine, of 496cc, is of their own production, with head shown, lateral valves of 45mm, forced lubrication with double automatic pump, crankcase cross-section, three-speed block gearbox and double cradle frame expansion brakes on the two wheels.

SANVENERO (1980–82)

Founded by Emilio Sanvenero, a Tuscan building contractor who had sponsored MBA and decided to set up his own manufacturing base with a view to competing in the 1981 125 and 500 Championships. When the MBA racing department was closed the following year Sanvenero effectively moved it to Follonica on the southern Tuscan coast. His 125cc was effectively a version on the MBA parallel twin, and the 500cc, a 120bhp square four, one version having stepped cylinders. Much was bought in: crankcase by Campagnolo, gearbox by CIMA, cranks by Hoeckle and pistons by Mahle, the frames by Nico Bakker. The riders were Carlo Perugini, Michel Frutschi and Guy Bertin. There was one 500 class win, at the boycotted French Nogaro Grand Prix for Frutschi, who finished fourteenth in the championship.

In the 125 class, Pier Paolo Bianchi brought home the best result with fourth in the championship in 1982, helped by a brace of second places. Team-mate Ricardo Tormo was fifth, and won in Belgium. After the team were bankrupted at the end of the year, Bianchi succeeded in obtaining some of the remaining motorcycles with which he ran in 1983, with three podium finishes.

SAR – *SEE* ELECT

SEGALE (1980–94)

A marque of which frustratingly little is known, given that they are still a Honda dealer in Vigevano in Pavia and occasionally offer specials, which are, in truth, accessorized standard models.

However, around 1980, they were building bespoke frames for Honda's new 16-valve fours, some kitted with parts from RSC (the HRC forerunner). Like Segoni (below), these used plated tubular frames, not unlike those of British frame-maker Harris. There was also a 700cc Honda single-powered version around 1990 for the then popular single-cylinder racing class and at least one Segale with a Suzuki GS1000 motor.

Most of the Segale were powered by twin-cam, 16-valve Honda fours.

BELOW: Although there is provision for a number plate, the Segale was built with endurance racing in mind.

SEGONI (1971–)

Two brothers from Florence, Giuliano and Roberto Segoni, built complete motorcycles with various engines, initially for racing. Like Segale (above), these used plated tubular frames not unlike those of British frame-maker Harris. Segoni's debut was in 1972 with a Laverda Segoni 750, ridden by Augusto Brettoni in the Imola 200 and then at the Bol d'Or. In 1973 and 1974, Segoni Corse was the only Italian team to finish the race.

In 1974, Segoni launched a street model powered by the Kawasaki Z900 engine of which fifty-two were sold. Between 1972 and 1978, Segoni Corse had entered in fourteen endurance races, including winning the Italian Juniors Championship with Gino Mandro on a Segoni-powered by a Suzuki 500 two-stroke twin.

When Giuliano died while test-riding a Segoni Kawasaki 900, the business was wound up, but was relaunched in 2015 by his son Lorenzo, alongside friend Tommaso Contri. The new Segoni G800 uses a 4-cylinder Kawasaki Z800 motor.

SEILING/SEI – *SEE* ALTEA

SENIOR (1913–14)

Motorcycles built by Bonzi & Marchi in Milan, using Moser singles of 296cc and 330cc. There are also references to a 500cc and V-twins.

SERTUM (1932–51)

Fausto Alberti started building engines for industrial use and boating. He launched his motorcycles under the Sertum (Garland, as presented to race winners) banner in 1932. The first model was a side-valve 175cc, quickly followed by the Batua, a 120cc two-stroke. Within two years, overhead- and side-valve, 250cc singles and 500cc parallel twins joined the range. Soon Sertum were one of the 'Big Five', alongside Benelli, Bianchi, Gilera and

Side-valve version of the Sertum motor.

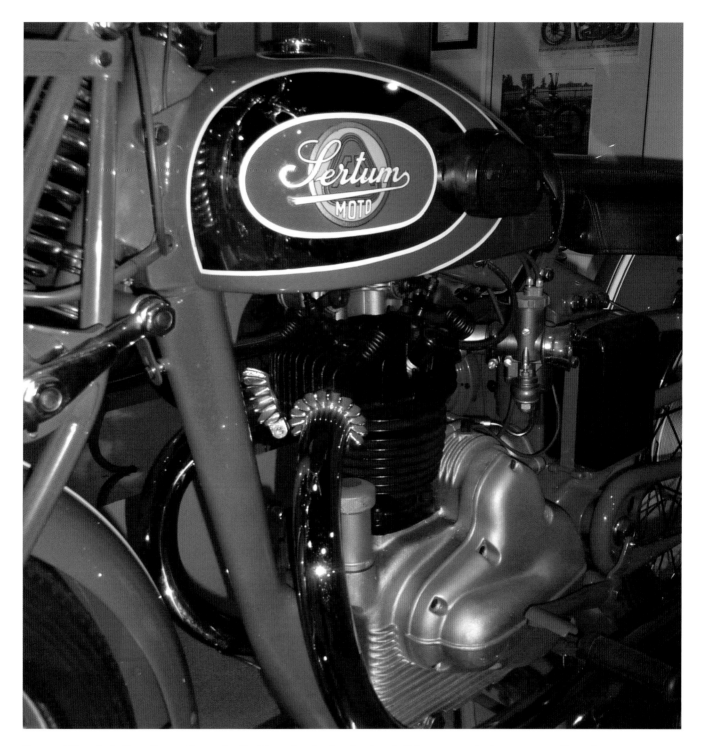

Some at Honda believe it was they who first imagined a 4-valve head: this pre-war Sertum proves otherwise.

Moto Guzzi. Competition success included five gold medals at the 1939 International Six Day Trials.

A new side-valve 500cc was developed for the military during the Second World War; it was civilianized for public sale in 1946, alongside a refreshed 250cc. There followed another two gold medals at the 1947 ISDT in Czechoslovakia. A new 250cc would bring further ISDT success but, like the other 'Big Five' (Moto Guzzi being an honourable exception), Sertum had assumed the post-war market would be like that of the 1930s, but found 500s especially just did not sell. In 1950, they showed a four-speed, 125cc, two-stroke, but there was no money left to put it into production. Sertum filed for bankruptcy and all assets were liquidated.

SESSA (1950–56)

Originally based in Varese, later moving to Milan, after which the motorcycles were badged as Moto Sessa. All used 147cc ILO motors.

SHIFTY (1975–78)

This was Ugo Grandis of Padua's attempt to convince the world that fitting Abarth-tuned Fiat 903cc and 1049cc fours into a motorcycle was a recipe for success. He was mistaken.

SIAMT (1906–14)

SIAMT (Società Italiana Automobili Motocicli) of Turin built Luigi Semeria's 260cc, 262cc and 344cc singles, as well as 494cc, 688cc and 731cc V-twins. Also a notable competition success.

SIATA – *SEE* DUCATI

SIMONCELLI (1927–35)

The Giacinto Simoncelli workshops were based in Verona. Initially, motorcycle production used two-stroke, 172cc Train engines. Later models switched to 173cc JAP side- and overhead-valve motors. From 1934, rear suspension was available.

SIMONETTA (1951–54)

Based in Milan, they built motorcycles with a 124cc, two-stroke motor.

SIMONINI (1970–83)

Founded by Enzo Simonini, late of Fiat, they offered Sachs two-stroke powered, off-road motorcycles of 50cc and 125cc, with five- and six-speed gearboxes, respectively. In 1974, the 50cc switched to Kreidler power, and there was a new 125cc and a 250cc with Simonini's own two-stroke engines. However, Sachs engine would still feature in the range, including the later liquid-cooled,

Simonini produced bike for 'Regolarità': timed trials with both long and short sections.

seven-speed, 250cc. By the late seventies, there was modest success in ISDTs and even an Italian junior championship, but sales were falling and Enzo Simonini was frustrated by his business partners. He continued in later years offering upgrade kits for two-stroke singles especially but it was not enough to save the business.

SIMPLEX (1921–50)

Based in Turin and, originally, they just built engines, followed by complete motorcycles with 123cc, two-stroke motors, with a horizontal cylinder. From 1927, there were overhead-valve 148cc, 173cc and, later, 246cc and 346cc singles. By 1937, there was at least one model with a 98cc Sachs motor, and a 500cc. The post-war relaunch was unsuccessful, with only a few motorcycles built.

STELLA (1925–28)

Based in Milan, they offered motorcycles with an overhead-valve, 173cc Blackburne engine.

STERZI (1939–62)

Based in Palazzolo sull'Oglio, north-west of Brescia, Vittorio Sterzi and his sons initially sold Dei and Bianchi motorcycles, as well as bicycles. They also worked with Sachs on their 98cc and 125cc engines. The eldest son, Aldo, had gained much experience with engines during the war and, around 1948, used this to establish a new factory in Brescia building complete motorcycles. The first model was based around a 125cc two-stroke but the most famous models came on-stream around 1953/4, with overhead-cam, four-strokes of 50cc and 65cc (the Pony), with 158cc and 173cc versions following. Equivalent two-strokes were also offered, most with forced air-fan cooling, including a scooter and three-wheeler.

Sterzi also assembled and supplied engines for others: the former for Hirth, the latter to Benotto, Girardengo and Bonvicini. Successful in competition and exporting, notably to Argentina, it is almost a mystery as to how the business collapsed in late 1950 and was gone just a few years later.

STILMA (1946–49)

Sociéta Torinese Industrie Lavorazioni Meccaniche Affini (STILMA, Turin) offered a 500cc overhead-valve single. One with engine number 003 was sold at a UK auction in 2011, with factory drawings and period documentation.

STORERO (1899–04)

Turin-built motorcycles and tricycle with a De Dion engine.

STUCCHI – *SEE* PRINETTI & STUCCHI

See image on page 164.

SUPERBA (1928–35)

Founded by the Casassa brothers near Genova, who produced motorcycles with overhead-valve 175s with Piazza and, later, JAP engines.

SUPERIOR (1934–36)

Motorcycles built by Giuseppe Milanaccio, with a 220cc engine with overhead camshaft.

SUPERMOTO (1925–26)

Powered by a side-valve 350cc, horizontal single-cylinder engine with forced cooling, built in Milan by Luigi Angelino.

SUPER ROYAL – *SEE* ROYAL

SVM (1984–87)

Based in Cesano Maderno, near Milan, formed from the ashes of SWM. They offered a moped, but mainly off-road, Villa-powered, two-strokes of 124cc and 329cc.

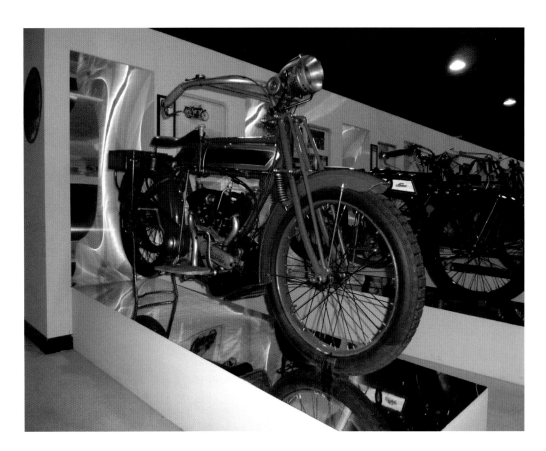

Stucchi, another long-forgotten marque, offered this V-twin. Like most motorcycles of its era, the gearbox was hand-change and the throttle a friction thumb lever on the right handlebar.

SWM (1971–84 / 2014–)

Speedy Working Motors was founded by Piero Sironi and Fausto Vergani in Milan. They could see that off-road motorcycling was rapidly switching to two-stroke power, when most European manufacturers were still offering four-strokes, even for competition. Observed trials, enduro, motocross and their off-road motorcycles were offered with Sachs engines of between 125cc and 350cc. From 1977, they switched to Rotax power, with capacities of up to 500cc. Joan Riudalbá, riding an SWM TF1, was Spanish Enduro Champion in 1980. The business failed in 1984, briefly revived as SVM, as above.

Armstrong of Bolton, England, bought the rights to the SWM XN Tornado, a Rotax-engined enduro machine of 350cc or 506cc. With CCM, Armstrong developed and marketed a military version, the MT-500, which was so successful that Harley-Davidson bought the manufacturing rights in 1986, and further developed the bike as the MT350E.

In 2014, Chinese investment allowed the name to be revived with facilities and designs previously sold under the Husqvarna banner, plus new purely road-going models. Despite the ownership, SWM continue to boast they are proud that their motorcycles are designed and built in northern Italy.

TARBO (1967–69)

TARtarini BOlogna, another marque founded by Leopoldo Tartarini (*see* Italjet) in collaboration with Jawa and using their 50cc and 125cc engines.

TAURA (1927–34)

Initially, motorcycles with a 175cc JAP engine and, from 1929, a 350cc overhead-cam and a 500cc side-valve. From 1930, Blackburne motors were also used in various capacities.

TAURUS – *SEE MG*

TGM (1971–83)

Trezzi and Marchesini, based in Parma, started with a Sachs-powered 50cc motocross bike that enjoyed some competition success. A Hiro-powered 125cc followed and then a 250cc with a Villa motor. In 1978, TGM finished twelfth (of thirty-nine classified) in the 125 World Motocross Championship with Michele Rinaldi.

THUNDER (1952–54)

Based in Reggio Emilia, they built a parallel twin 125cc or 127cc four-stroke that was far too expensive to survive.

TITAN CYCLE (1973–90)

Off-road motorcycles, 125cc Sachs-powered variants used the Morini model names of Sbarazzina and Corsarino models under licence. Also, Franco Morini-powered mopeds.

TM (1968–)

Founded by Claudio Flenghi and Francesco Battistelli in Pesaro and named after their sons – Thomas and Mirko. The aim was building off-road competition machines, initially inspired by Yamaha. The first model was a 125cc two-stroke with six-speed gearbox, but the range became almost bewildering in its options, including Supermoto and two- and four-stroke engines, which are also sold for Karting. Despite being expensive, TM has always allowed privateers to be competitive in off-road sport and the company still takes competition success very seriously.

TOMMASI (1926–27)

Genoa-built motorcycles equipped with 123ccx two-stroke Della Ferrera engines and, apparently, a 246cc model created by using two 123cc engines.

TOMASELLI (1931–39)

Ugo Tomaselli's Turin workshop used 173cc to 498cc JAP engines.

TRAIN ITALIA (1932–35)

Subsidiary of the French Train engine manufacturer, based in Turin. Established by Giuseppe Navone, who offered complete motorcycles with the 100cc Train engine.

TRANS-AMA (1978–85)

Based in Pesaro with the aim of building off-road motorcycles for the USA market – initially, 50cc, 125cc and 250cc in motocross and enduro versions. The 50cc motor was from Minarelli, all the others from Hiro. Particularly interesting was the 320cc trial model, again with a Hiro engine, developed by Sammy Miller. This had a curved spine frame to allow the fuel tank to be under the seat. Launched in 1981, it was more of a curiosity and not a sales success. Trans-Ama tried their luck with children's motorcycles, again using Minarelli engines, but it was not enough to save the company.

TRESPIDI (1925–34)

Paolo Trespidi's workshop in Stradella, south of Milan. The first model used Trespidi's own a 250cc three-port, two-stroke engine, followed in 1929 by a 175cc.

TRUBBIANI (1948–52)

Giuseppe Trubbiani's workshop in Potenza, south of Ancona, built a handful of motorcycles with ILO 125cc two-stroke engines and a three-speed gearbox.

TURKLLEIMER – *SEE* ASTRA

UNIMOTO (1980–88)

Formed from the ashes of moped producer Milani in Longiano, west of Rimini, Unimoto too started out with Minarelli-powered mopeds. But, in 1982, Unimoto absorbed Aspes Moto, allowing it to offer 125cc on and off-road 125cc two-strokes using Tau motors. The ultimate, 22bhp, versions arrived circa 1984, with liquid-cooling and monoshock rear suspension, as the Squalo GP roadster and the TK 125 off-roader.

UNIMOTO ITALY

Unimoto Mototopo

Engine: single cylinder, two stroke. Cubic capacity: 79.5 cc. Bore and stroke: 48 x 44 mm. Maximum output: 8 bhp (DIN) at 9500 rmp. Compression ratio: 11 1. Dellorto PHBH 30 BS carburettor, petroil premix lubricat at 2³/₀, kickstart.

Transmission: primary drive by gea final by chain, wet multiplate clutch, six speed gearbox.

Ignition: electronic.

Frame: tubular.

Suspension: front: hydraulic fork; ar: swinging arm fork with shock absorbers.

Tyres: front and rear 21 x 12-8.

Brakes: front and rear drums.

Weight: 184.9 lbs (84 kg).

Max speed: not stated.

Unimoto - Aspes - Via Emilia 1853 - 47020 Longiano (FO).

Unimoto Squalo 125

Engine: single cylinder, two stroke. Cubic capacity: 124.5 cc. Bore and stroke: 56 x 50.6 mm. Maximum output: 22.5 bhp (DIN) ot 7800 rmp. Compression ratio: .3 : 1. Dellorto PHBH 28 BS carburettors, kickstart.

Transmission: primary drive by gears,final by chain, wet multiplate clutch, six speed gearbox.

Ignition: electronic.

Frame: duplex tubular cradle.

Suspension: front: Marzocchi telehydrau fork; rear: swinging arm fork with shock absorber.

Tyres: front 3.00 x 18; rear 3.50 x 18.

Brakes: front disc; rear drum.

Weight: 242.4 lbs (110 kg).

Max speed: not stated.

Unimoto - Aspes - Via Emilia 1853 - 47020 Longiano (FO).

Unimoto Enduro TK 125

Engine: single cylinder, two stroke. Cubic capacity: 124.5 cc. Bore and stroke: 56 x 50.6 mm. Maximum output: 22.5 bhp (DIN) at 7800 rmp. Compression ratio: 14.3 : 1. Dellorto PHBH 28 BS carburettors, kickstart.

Transmission: primary drive by gears, final by chain, wet multiplate clutch, six speed gearbox.

Ignition: electronic.

Frame: duplex tubular cradle.

Suspension: front: Marzocchi telehydraulic fork; rear: swinging arm fork with shock absorber.

Tyres: front 2.75 x 21; rear 4.10 x 18.

Brakes: front disc; rear drum.

Weight: 244.6 lbs (111 kg).

Max speed: not stated.

Unimoto - Aspes - Via Emilia 1853 - 47020 Longiano (FO).

104

Unimoto offered remarkably high specification 125s.

VAGA (1925–35)

Based in Milan, with Mario Vaga offering mainly British-engined 175s. The first used a two-stroke Blackburne engine and a three-speed Burman gearbox. Later models used four-stroke JAP and Sturmey Archer and, in 1930, there was a CF overhead-cam version (see also CF and Fusi entries).

VAGHI (1920–24)

Milan-based, they made lightweight tricycles and cars powered by V-twin, four-strokes. There are suggestions a motorcycle was also available.

VALENTI (1978–84)

Milan-based marque that initially offered 125cc and 25cc two-stroke trial bikes and, later, Honda-powered 80cc children's models followed.

VANONI (1926–27)

500cc single-cylinder with overhead-camshaft built in Gallarate by Nino Vanoni.

VAMPA (1927–30)

Attractive vertical single, 125cc two-stroke with external flywheel and two-speed gearbox built in Modena.

VASCHETTO (1936–38)

Built in Turin by Giuseppe Vaschetto; available with 250cc and 500cc Mercury engines.

VASSENA (1926–29)

125cc two-stroke with horizontal cylinder and Ideal two-speed gearbox from Pietro Vassena, based in Lecco, on Lake Como. Some were sold under the Faini banner (see Faini). After the war, Vassena designed engines for Rumi.

VEROS – *SEE GARANZINI*

VERTEMATI/VOR (1998–2010)

Founded near Milan by brothers Alvaro and Guido Vertemati to build off-road competition motorcycles, relying on their experience of motocross and as importers of Swedish Husaberg off-roaders.

Various models were offered, all large-capacity four-strokes but, in 2002, the company was absorbed into the Mondial group and relaunched as VOR (Vertemati Off-Road Racing). The brothers relaunched independently as Vertemati Racing in collaboration with Benelli at first, but the promised independently produced models failed to appear in 2010.

VG (1931–35)

Vittorio Grilli built a limited number of motorcycles equipped with JAP engines.

VICENTINI (1925–26)

250cc two-stroke diesel motor equipped with a supercharger cylinder. The name was revived post-war for a range of lightweights of up to 125cc, built in Argentina using Minarelli two-stroke engines.

VILLA (1968–88)

Founded by Francesco Villa in Modena and later, when working with his brother Walter, based in Bologna, initially they built just engines. Francesco had a glorious racing history behind him, notably with Ducati and later Mondial, especially where he won the 125 class of the Italian senior championship four times. In 1965, Francesco conquered again and took his final national 125 title on the two-stroke Mondial and immediately penned a narrower and lighter engine version. Despite Mondial being reluctant to race it under their own name, a number of the so-called Beccaccino (snipe) were sold to trusted individuals, including Francesco's brother, Walter. He used it to take the 125 title for Mondial yet again in 1966 and, unsurprisingly, Mondial were happy to take the credit. In truth, however, the motorcycle was really the start of the Villas' own company.

The remarkable Villa 250 V4, outlawed before it could be raced.

In 1966, with the Villa brothers in joint collaboration, after producing a few prototypes in 1965, they presented two new 125cc and 250cc motorcycles: both two-strokes with twin cylinders inclined forward by 30 degrees. The 125cc was claimed to give 30bhp at 14,000rpm, up 30 per cent from the Mondial single. The 250cc had water-cooled barrels but a finned, air-cooled head and promised 48bhp at 11,500rpm. The 250cc had a front-mounted disc brake – all other brakes being drum.

But the Villas wanted to carry on racing, so they sold the designs to the Spanish Montesa factory on the condition that they would campaign them in the world championship with the Villa's retained as riders for 1966 and 1967. The project suffered from reliability issues and, by 1968, Francesco was racing a 125 Villa again, with Walter joining him in 1969 on Villa 125s and 250s.

Francesco thought, quite rationally, if the 250cc twin lacked speed, the answer was to double the 125cc up to create a 250 V4. Early in 1969, Villa's 250cc Grand Prix engine was essentially two air-cooled 125cc twins of 43 × 43mm bore/stroke mounted one above the other on a common crankcase at an included angle of 30 degrees, the crankshafts being connected via a coupling gear. As well as serving as the primary drive, the latter also drove the ignition unit and oil pump. Drive was transmitted via a dry clutch to the eight-speed gearbox, and the engine/transmission unit was housed in a heavily gusseted du-plex loop frame. Ceriani supplied the front forks and rear dampers, and there were Fontana brakes on both wheels.

Tragically for the Villas, their new baby arrived just in time to be rendered obsolete by the FIM's rule change limiting the 250 class to a maximum of two cylinders from the start of the 1970 season. Nevertheless, the brothers decided to try and race it at least once and entered the untried V4 in the Italian Grand Prix at Monza. After running erratically during practice, the V4 was put to one side and Walter rode a rotary valve single that had been brought as backup.

The sole V4 prototype was later sold to the Bombardier Corporation in Canada and is now owned by a Swiss enthusiast. One man who had admired it during his time working for Moto Villa was Giovanni Galafassi, creator of the faithful replica photographed here. 'I thought it was a tragedy it never raced,' said Galafassi, interviewed by Alan Cathcart for his *Classic Racer* article on the Villa V4 (March/April 2010 edition) 'that the FIM bureaucrats destroyed the heritage of Italian motorcycle culture represented by machines like the Villa and 4-cylinder Benelli, in favour of creating a monomarca [single marque] class for Yamaha twins.'

Riding the Villa V4 recreation for the very first time since its completion, Alan Cathcart found that the engine started pulling strongly from just under 8,000rpm on its way to a peak of 12,500 revs. 'I can't deny that seeing the V4 running on the track, after ten years spent in the workshop building it, gives me a lot of satisfaction,' said Galafassi.

Francesco Villa could now be considered one of the most experienced technicians of two-stroke engines in the world. Sitting in his workshop in the Via Pistoia Vaciglio, on the outskirts of Modena, he must have realized that the Japanese might have managed to get road racing rules changed to suit themselves, off-road two-strokes were only just starting to become popular. Villa had been selling 50cc and 125cc off-road bikes with Franco Morini engines since 1969, but, for 1972, he built a limited number of motocross 250s, designated CRs, with a single-cylinder, two-stroke engine that Villa had designed for road racing. The problem with putting this into production was that it proved impossible to fit a kick start, but that did not stop Italo Forni winning thirty-six of the thirty-eight races it competed in during 1972.

The production models were offered with both 250cc and 450cc versions; initially at least, they were very much aimed at professional racers. The Carabela factory in Mexico was so impressed by the CR engine that it began buying Villa engines for its own motorcycles. This would prove to be another valuable income stream – not just suppling engines to other motorcycle builders, but also to Karters.

Meanwhile the production Villas were continually upgraded, especially components: Ceriani forks, Marzocchi dampers and Campagnolo magnesium hubs were standard by 1974. But they were not elitist or monomaniacal – there were still Franco Morini children's bikes and occasional road-racing bikes, especially 50s and 125s. The former was especially successful – Claudio Lusuardi used one to win the Italian 50cc Championship in 1974, 1980 and 1982.

The end of 1974 brought a new range of off-road models, the FV range, which again evolved year on year. There were eventually 250cc, 350cc, 360cc and 380cc engines, available in both motocross and enduro (so road-legal) versions. Highly successful in completion, a Villa FV won the 1976 Junior Motocross 250 Championship. From 1979, a 480FX version was offered with a near 490cc capacity.

Liquid-cooling arrived first on the 125cc with the radiator above the front mudguard initially, but soon relocated to a more conventional position. From 1981, six-speed gearboxes started to appear. The following year was the first for monoshocks.

From 1980 to 1984, Villa offered a TT4. The Italian National Championship from 1980 on adopted what amounted to the Formula TT rules, where the Isle of Man ran world championships based on production engines. The smallest class (Formula 3) was for two-strokes

The very narrow angle between the cylinders allowed good packaging and use of two Villa 125 twins to create the 250.

of up to 250cc, and four-strokes up to 400cc. The Italian manufacturers protested to the FMI that this would leave no national championship that a 125cc could hope to win, an incredibly important part of the domestic market. So the FMI added a TT4 class, for motorcycles with a production engine (not necessarily a production chassis) of up to 125cc. The Villa effort, with the single-cylinder, air-cooled 125cc engine, won the Italian TT4 Championship in 1981, 1982 and 1983, in the hands of Gianola, Cadalora and Gibertini, respectively.

Inevitably, this meant Villa needed a production road-going 125cc to sell on the back of their racing success. From 1982, this was, initially, the half-faired Daytona – a sports option – and the rather plainer Italia. There then followed the Paso-style FB Mondial 125 Super Sport with a fully enclosed fairing, very much a vanity project for Count Boselli, one of the brothers (Fratelli) Boselli that were the FB in Mondial. Developed and built by Moto Villa, production was halted shortly after it began, with a limited series of only twenty units being built.

But even this willingness to embrace new markets and innovate could not save Villa from the sheer numbers and low prices of the Japanese models, and Villa called it a day in 1988, although they remain as a spares' supplier to this day.

VILLANI (1925–37)

Andrea Villani in Bologna offered a two-stroke, single-cylinder 175cc and, by doubling it up, a parallel twin 350cc.

VITTORIA (1931–78)

Motorcycles built in Vittorio Veneto. Sachs engines of 98cc, JAP of 175cc and 250cc, Küchen of 350cc and 500cc, and Rudge Pythons of 500cc. Post-war there were mostly mopeds, scooters and lightweights, all powered by two-strokes mostly from Sachs.

VOLTA (1902–07)

The Dalifol French steam engine, built under license in Italy by Volta, was equipped with a central boiler, a coal burner and a single-cylinder engine with direct transmission.

VOLUGRAFO (1939–42)

Miniature, small-wheel motorcycle, produced in Turin during the Second World War, for the paratroopers of the Italian Army; powered by a 98cc two-stroke with a two-speed gearbox.

VYRUS (2003–15)

Vyrus founder, Ascanio Rodorigo, started his motorcycle engineering career as a mechanic in the Bimota racing team in 1973, alongside the legendary Massimo Tamburini. After Tamburini's departure, Bimota suffered one of the first of its financial crises and stopped racing. Moved to the production line, a bored Rodorigo handed in his notice and, in 1985, started his own company under the ARP banner (his initials) in Rimini, offering special parts for race or road, including frames. Inevitably, this included working on Bimota Tesis, the chassis notoriously difficult to set up for racing. Eventually, Rodorigo became convinced he could do better and, in September 2002, decided to do so.

ARP's part-time helpers included Dervis Macrelli, who had worked on frames with Tamburini and was the working at the Cagiva Research Centre that devel-

The Vyrus on the road. Phil Read junior raced one.
MYKEL NICOLAOU

Despite the Bimota badge, Vyrus built the Tesi 3D, having learnt much from setting up the original model behind.

Rear suspension is
surprisingly
conventional, without a
rising rate linkage.

oped the Ducati 916, MV Agusta F4 and Cagiva grand prix 500. Styling was Rodorigo's work with help from ex-Ducati and Pierre Terblanche's designer Sam Matthews. Ideas would be emailed between the two until Matthews could produce CAD drawings for Rodorigo to turn into a show bike. The bodywork was created in clay, working until three in the morning. It was at this point, Rodorigo decided that to be determined to work this hard, meant he must have a virus, a virus like no other: so he spelt it Vyrus.

That first Vyrus 984 made its debut at the Padova Show in January 2003, powered by a Ducati 900SS Desmodue engine, upgraded to a similar specification to the bike ARP had been racing with success in Super Twins. The 984cc engine was a known baseline for ARP, important given that Rodorigo had imagined building either to order or in small batches. In fact he was faced with hundreds of potential orders, necessitating homologation and series production. The result was not just a radical motorcycle, but also the lightest twin-cylinder sports bike on sale. Over the next three years, around seventy Vyrus were delivered, twenty-five of which were badged as Bimota 2Ds and sold through the relaunched Bimota dealer network.

The development process included racing in European twin-cylinder classes, ridden by Gianluca Villa, nephew of the late four-time world champion, Walter. Inevitably, Desmoquattro versions followed, including the 2010 on 987 C3 4V, powered by a 211bhp supercharged Ducati 1198cc motor. Tom Cruise sang the praises of his Vyrus on the *Top Gear* television show in 2010, probably the best advertising it is possible to generate.

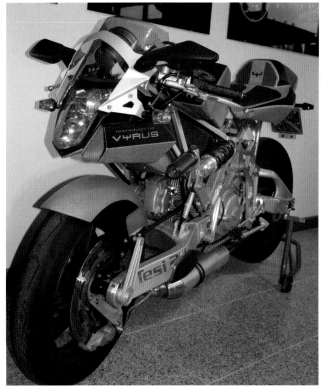

This looks almost identical to the original Tesi set up, but is far easier to get the best from.

In 2011, Vyrus ambitiously announced a kit to build entries for Moto2, the world championship then using the Honda CBR600 motor as the control power plant. This was the 986 M2 and differed from previous Vyrus or Bimota hub-steered bikes in that, instead of using mechani-

Two of Italy's most original motorcycles – the Vyrus with a Ducati 750SS. MYKEL NICOLAOU

cal steering rods and linkages to steer, a pair of hydraulic pistons was used. New bodywork used the Honda motor as a stressed member, the carbon fibre styled by Yutaka Igarashi and Sam Matthews. Unfortunately, despite Vyrus running it in the 2015 Moto2 European Championship with Bradley Ray, there were no serious takers. Sadly, Vyrus seem to have disappeared shortly thereafter.

WOLSIT (1910–68)

Legnano factory initially planning to build British Wolsey cars under licence. That project went into liquidation in 1907 (the history of the marque is very much bankruptcy and rebirth) and, from 1910, Wolsit were offering 3.5bhp bikes with three-speed gearboxes. From 1932, the name Wolsit reappeared on a bicycle equipped with an NSU engine mounted above the front wheel. Post-war, the factory moved to Milan offering cyclemotors with Cucciolo, Mosquito and Sachs engines. From the 1960s, there were mopeds and, finally, a 175cc for 1967.

ZENIT (1953–56)

Pontedera factory established by Bruno Morelli, using French engines: a 160cc two-stroke and a 175cc four-stroke. Not much to go on, but it is nice to finish an A–Z of Italian motorcycles with a Z!

APPENDIX: THOSE WHO ALSO SERVED

As noted in the introduction, this is an A-Z of Italian motorcycles but for the sake of completeness, even those Italian factories that I believe solely built cyclemotors, mopeds or scooters are included here. Some of the names did produce motorcycles but if it proved impossible to establish where the factory was based, they are omitted from the A–Z and listed here. Some may have been firms that once had high hopes, others simply an individual with a well-equipped workshop who fancied seeing their own name on a fuel tank. If you ever are fortunate enough to discover a previously unheard of Italian motorcycle, hopefully its name is at least on this list and offers a start to researching its history.

Abignente	BRM	Furetto
Abra	BS Villa	Gaio
Acsa	BSU	Galator
AD	Cabrera	Gallmotor
Aguzzi	Cappello	Garaffa
Algat	Carda	Garlaschelli
Alkro	Carniti	Gatti
Almia	Carrù	GC
Alpina	Cavicchioli	Ghiaroni
Arzani	Cicala	GKD
Ariz	Cigno	Grassetti
Astro	Cima	GRG
B & P	Cislaghi	GS motors
Bardone	CMK	Guaraldi
Bantam	CMO	Guaraschi
Baroni	Colella	Guizzo
Bazzoni	Coppi	HM
Beccaccino/Bettocchi	Construzione Meccaniche G. Viviani	Idra
Beccarta	Cozzo	IGM
Bertoni	Di Blasi	Imperia
Bimm	Di Pietro's	Imprese generali
BMG	Dik-Dik	Industria motori
BMM	Dionisi	Innocenti
Boassi	Eolo	Intramotor
Bottari	EST	Invicta
Breda	Fuchs/Tappelia-Fuchs	Iprem
Brena	Fulgor	Iris

Italjap	MP	San Cristoforo
Italkart	MR	Sancineto
Italmoto	MT34	Santamaria
Janga	Nassetti	Scarab
Jenis	Necchi	Siat
Lancia	Negrini	Signorelli
Landi	NVB	Sillaro
Lem motor	Maccaniche benesi	SIM
Leone	Olmo	Simonetta
Low	Oman	Sirio
Lucini	Omer	Sirtori
Lupetto	Orani	Spaviero
Lusardi	Oscar	Sumco
Luzi	Parvus	Tansini
MR	Passoni	Tappella
Mafalda	Paglianti	Tauma
Maino	Pegaso	Technomoto
Maiolina	Peripoli	Terra modena
Mafarda	PGO	Testi
Mantovani	PG-Parena	TGR
Maranello Moto	Piaggio	Tigli
Marchi & Fabbri	Piermattei	Torpado
Marchitelli	Piviere	Tresoldi
Marini	Pizeta	Trevisan
Martina	Plico	Twm
Mazzucchelli	Polenghi	UFO
MBM	Polini	Ultra
MBR	Pony	Vamam
Menani	Rapid	Vecchietti
Memzzi electra	REC	Vega
Mengoli	Reggioli	Velox technica
Milani	Remondini	Velta
Minimarcellino	Ringhini	Veltro
Minizeta	Riva	Verga
Monte rosa	Rivara	Viberti
Moretti	Rizzato	Vicini
Motauto	Romano	Viking
Moto Biros	Romeo	Vi-Vi
Moto Futuro	Rond sachs	Wilier
Moto Graziella	Rosetta	WRM
Moto Italia	Sacom	Zannetti
Motoclipper	Saletta	Zepa
Motoflash	Sama	Zeta
Motomec	Samp	Zoppoli
Motron	Sanciome	

INDEX

RELATED TITLES FROM CROWOOD

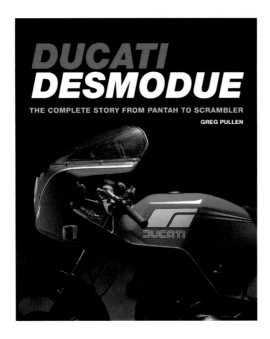

Ducati Desmodue
ISBN 978 1 84797 901 8

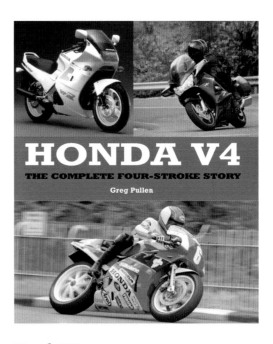

Honda V4
ISBN 978 1 84797 754 0

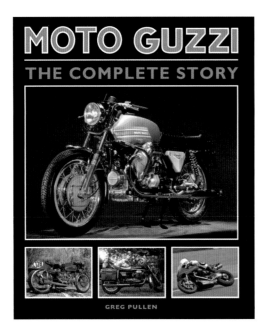

Moto Guzzi
ISBN 978 1 84797 576 8

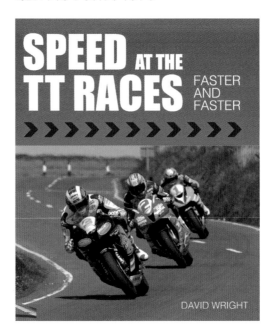

Speed at the TT Races
ISBN 978 1 78500 298 4

www.crowood.com